Call Light

By J. M. Frollo

DORRANCE
PUBLISHING CO
EST. 1920
PITTSBURGH, PENNSYLVANIA 15238

The contents of this work, including, but not limited to, the accuracy of events, people, and places depicted; opinions expressed; permission to use previously published materials included; and any advice given or actions advocated are solely the responsibility of the author, who assumes all liability for said work and indemnifies the publisher against any claims stemming from publication of the work.

Dorrance Publishing Co
585 Alpha Drive
Pittsburgh, PA 15238
Visit our website at *www.dorrancebookstore.com*

ISBN: 978-1-6495-7034-5
EISBN: 978-1-6491-3879-8

For all my colleagues united by wings:

Thank you for inspiring me to write the humor we encounter regularly and please continue to share your funny, beautiful, and fascinating stories.

Contents

Introduction

Several years ago, I was working as a consultant for math education, and the position required that I commute by air travel twice per week. When I first started flying between Pittsburgh and NYC regularly, I was nervous about every aspect of the experience: arriving on time to the airport, possibly setting off the metal detector at security, flying through turbulence, and losing my checked bag. I rarely traveled by plane, only for destinations that were too far to drive to and even then, flights were few and far between.

But after the first few weeks of navigating airports and airplanes, the back and forth travel became part of my routine. I learned how to expedite my time at the TSA security checkpoints, I had a better understanding of the boarding process, and I knew exactly which chimes on the airplane meant that I had about 15 more minutes before I had to put my laptop away for landing. Maybe I had finally got the hang of it all.

Air travel had become my new normal for commuting; instead of jumping into a car, I was jumping on a plane — it was becoming second nature. My nervousness gradually dissipated as the process became more familiar with each flight. I started actually enjoying travel. I was no longer the person holding up the security line because I forgot to empty out my pockets before going through the metal detector. The noise of the landing gear lowering wasn't startling me awake anymore. Surprisingly, I started to feel more at ease hearing the white noise of the purring airplane engines up in the air than I did hearing car horns honking on the ground in New York City. Instead of feeling anxious entering an airport, I felt comfortable, like I was going to a place of calm.

I loved the work that I did in education, but each week became more stressful and less rewarding than the previous one. The frustration came to a head, and I was about to burst after having one of the most frustrating and exhausting work weeks. My friend Andrea, a flight attendant, reached out to meet me while on layover in NYC.

During our time together, she forced me to gaze into a figurative mirror and realize how miserable I was in my career. She suggested I consider applying to be a flight attendant. "I think it would be perfect for you," she said convincingly. In conjunction with the frustrating workdays and the come-to-Jesus talk with Andrea, the final straw was the realization that to destress before every Friday night flight home, a couple martinis were necessary, not optional. That's when I knew it was time to take a leap of faith with a new career, hoping that I'd find something I loved doing that wouldn't drive me to drink.

While in flight, I thought more about what Andrea had said to me. I loved being on an airplane because the stress and anxiety of my daily grind were literally miles below. I would notice that the anxiousness seemed to lessen once I was up in the air. I pictured myself being a flight attendant: I could spend my days flying and I could spend my time on layovers exploring new places! The idea did sound enticing. What would it hurt to apply for a position?

Well, the stars aligned, and I decided that I'd take my teacher hat off to become a student again. I would be heading to flight attendant training to learn all about the industry. I knew I loved to travel, and I didn't much mind the idea of serving people in the sky. I was excited that my lifelong learning would continue, though. Now, instead of focusing on mathematics, I'd be switching my studies to people and world cultures. Besides, I was already accustomed to the flight attendant lifestyle by staying in hotels and living out of a suitcase regularly with my current position, so why not jump in feet first?

What I hadn't considered was that even though I was ready to be a full-time flyer, passengers were still just like I had been at the beginning of my commuting period. For others, the idea of air travel isn't quite as thrilling. Many passengers are focused on making sure they have everything they need and that they're following all the rules so the whole experience goes smoothly. Did I remember my passport? Who has the boarding passes? Were all the liquids under three ounces? All of these are the same types of concerns that I had at the start of my consulting job.

For me, when that anxiety finally went away while commuting, and even more so when I became a flight attendant, I developed this burning wondering: What the hell happens to people when they pass through the sliding glass doors of an airport? Is there something more to that breathtaking gust of wind that immediately hits as a flyer enters an airport? I have a theory that when travelers pass through the sliding doors, they're actually passing through a vortex of senselessness that strips them from their common sense, common courtesies, and basic abilities to reason and problem solve. Too far-fetched?

I've yet to find anyone who has been able to disprove my theory! If I were to tell you that the majority of our country's population has significant trouble with, specifically, the first ten letters of the English alphabet and counting numbers up to 50, you'd laugh in my face and tell me I was crazy. My rebuttal: Of approximately the last 2,000 flights I've flown, I can count on one hand the number of flights when every single passenger boarded and sat in the correct seat. And how do passengers identify their correct seats? They apply proficiencies in counting to 50 and recognition of the letters A through J. Our population certainly possesses basic skills learned in kindergarten, but there's just something about the whole air travel experience that seems to find a way to stupefy many passengers, and that's why I knew I needed to write this book.

Toward the end of my time as a consultant, I began writing down short stories and events that I witnessed while either sitting in the airport or while flying on planes. As I dove into aviation as a flight attendant, I continued keeping track of those stories, sharing them with friends and family on social media, and recalling them at gatherings. I realized that the reason why everyone enjoyed these airline-themed vignettes was because they could all find a way to relate to the humanity that grounds the stories and the characters in them.

In our daily lives, we see people make careless mistakes and we can usually all laugh about them together. We see people accentuate their entitlement and find ourselves collectively rolling our eyes, grateful for the gift of humility. And we see real emotions like sadness and excitement that trigger us to offer support and celebrate successes. Those moments of humanity don't just disappear when it comes to flying. If anything, they are heightened and, frankly, more interesting than ever. These moments led me to a realization: The challenges I face working as a flight attendant aren't much different from the challenges that I faced when teaching children. So, maybe that's why so many flight attendants are ex-educators!

In every story, the names of the real characters and their specific flight information have been removed or changed to protect identities, but there's no doubt in my mind that you know these people. You may not know their names or what specific flight they flew, but you will undoubtedly recognize these passengers. Let's face facts, you might have been one of them—I admit that I certainly am guilty, myself. We all have our flaws, that's what makes us human and interesting. And while I'm always trying to think of ways to bring more kindness to the table, I must admit that I enjoy a snarky "clap back" just like the next person. Who doesn't want to see the troublemakers get what they deserve?!

In recalling and sorting through the many memorable stories that I wanted to share, I knew that I wanted to let others experience the same range of feelings that I did as each scenario occurred. I wanted readers to have a sneak peek into the view of the flight attendant and shed light on some of the strange and funny things that occur on airplanes. Whether a story highlights a shocking action, a quick-witted response, or a beautiful act of kindness, its sole function is to celebrate our strengths, learn from our flaws and remind us that we should do our best to always go through life with a sense of humor.

Airline Jargon

B elow is a list of some frequently used terms of the airline industry that may help in understanding some components of the stories ahead.

Arming: Placing the aircraft door arming lever into the emergency mode so that if the door should be opened the evacuation slide will deploy

Base: The city where a flight attendant begins and ends every rotation

Boarding: Entering an aircraft

Briefing: A short meeting with members of the flight crew regarding a variety of information about the flight

Carry-On Baggage: Any baggage or items that a passenger takes onto the plane and claims responsibility of for the entire duration of the flight experience

Checked Baggage: Any baggage that is kept below the passenger cabin in the cargo area that a passenger is responsible for reclaiming in the baggage claim area

Deadheading: When a flight attendant rides in a passenger seat on a flight to be positioned for the next working leg of a trip or to be returned to base

Deplaning: Exiting an aircraft

Disarming: Placing the door lever into normal operational mode so that if the door should be opened, the evacuation slide will not deploy

FAA or Federal Aviation Administration: The US government organization that creates the rules regarding safety that flight attendants must abide by and enforce

Flight Deck: Where the pilots sit and fly the plane (also referred to as the cockpit)

Fuselage: The long, main portion of the airplane that houses the passenger cabin; The wings, engines and tail are all attached to this part of the plane

Galley: The area(s) of an aircraft where food and service supplies are stored

Jumpseat: Fold-down seats usually located near air-craft exits, which flight attendants must occupy during takeoff and landing

Jetbridge: A connector between the terminal and the aircraft with a tunnel-like appearance

Lavatory: The airplane's restroom

Layover: The period spent in a city between flights

Rotation: The itinerary of flights that a flight attendant will work with the same colleagues over the course of one day or multiple days. Each itinerary begins and ends in the base city.

Seat Set: One side of a row of seats; For example: Seats ABC on the left side of the aircraft are one seat set and seats DEF on the right side of the aircraft are another seat set.

Taxiing: When an airplane drives around prior to takeoff or after landing.

Call Light

Age Discrimination

I was five months into my new career as a flight attendant. I still had excitement as I showed up to work bright-eyed and bushy-tailed, ready to transport people all over the United States. Yet, I was also very timid. I feared upsetting a passenger by saying the wrong thing, forgetting a proper protocol of service, or even — heaven forbid — spilling something on someone. I was determined to be "by-the-book" while following the airline's standards for safety and service, because I was on my way to graduating the probationary period for new flight attendants and nothing would keep me from crossing that finish line.

I had been sitting in the airport for approximately four hours and the flight was supposed to have left three hours earlier. Delays happen and they are rarely fun to deal with. In this case, passengers were worried about missing connecting flights, everyone was restless from sitting in the uncomfortable airport seats, and patience ran thin when the delayed status continued to roll back the departure time without any end in sight. These types of lengthy delays weren't very common, thankfully, but when they happened, the flight attendants had to be sure their tanks of kindness, patience, and tolerance were completely full, if not over-flowing. So, I treated myself to an iced coffee to boost my caffeine and overall mood for what could be a potentially trying flight with grumpy passengers.

The aircraft arrived, deplaned, and received a quick cleaning and catering. Boarding was ready to begin. As part of the service offered in the first-class cabin, while on the ground and prior to departure, the passengers were offered a beverage of their choice to enjoy while the rest of the passengers boarded. Many of our passengers took advantage of this service to start their morning with a cup of coffee or juice, while other passengers aimed to take the edge off with a glass of red wine or a cocktail. All of these were acceptable requests any time of day, until the person requesting alcohol appeared to be under the legal drinking age.

I headed into the first-class cabin with my paper and pen, prepared to jot down a plethora of cocktail orders and to expedite the distribution of these pre-flight beverages. With Air Traffic Control having given us our new slotted departure time, I knew we would have more than enough time to offer this service without delaying our departure any further. I still liked to be efficient, though. No one likes to be held up from boarding with their luggage in tow. I started with rows 1 and 2. White wines, red wines, vodka-soda-limes—all orders that I expected. Then, I reached Mr. Big Shot in the third row.

Mr. Big Shot wore a buttoned-down, pale-blue and white checkered shirt tucked into a pair of tan khaki pants that laid over a pair of tasseled loafers. His dark brown hair was combed over the same way his mom probably used to part it for him not too long ago. His most notable physical feature, however, was his sweet, little baby face; he looked like he couldn't have been any older than fifteen. I remember wondering if he was even old enough to have a driver's license, let alone whether he was old enough to consume alcohol.

He had his tray table laid across his lap. On it sat his hybrid laptop/tablet with the keyboard attached and his cell phone laying by its side as if to appear to be engaged in business that required every electronic device he owned. Perhaps he had the idea that if he looked important and busy, he would be perceived to be a young businessman, and all young professionals are at least 21 years old, right? Something seemed off about the whole situation.

I stepped up to this young professional and asked him if he would care for a beverage before we departed. To my very real surprise, he put on a well-rehearsed show. He was heavily invested—acting distracted—in whatever he was pretending to accomplish on his computer screen and pulled himself away for only the few seconds necessary to say, "Yes. You can get me a rum and Coke." Then he dove right back into his computer screen.

Oh, can I? I decided to keep that comment to myself. Instead, I took a moment to pause and breathe through all the entitlement that so easily spewed out of his mouth, then proceeded to respond, "I would be happy to get that for you, sir. I just need to take a quick peek at your ID." Without hesitation, Mr. Big Shot started with an innocent excuse, "Oh, my ID is up in the overhead bin. It's in my wallet inside of my backpack. Do I still need to get it down?"

First sign that he wasn't 21: he used the "my ID is up there" excuse. This is more common than you would think. I didn't believe him, and I was squashing it. "Yes, unfortunately, I do have to check it quickly. If you want to go ahead and grab that while I'm taking all of the rest of the orders, I can check it for you on my way back, and then I'll get that drink right out to you."

Annoyed that I wasn't giving in, he angrily raised his voice, "This is crazy. We've been delayed four hours, and you want to slow us down even more by holding up the boarding process for everyone standing behind you. Just so I can get my license out just to prove I'm 21 years old? This is ridiculous."

It was *absolutely* ridiculous. It was ridiculous that I had to engage in back-and-forth banter with a child who genuinely thought the battle was worth fighting. If you had to wait an hour for your table at a restaurant would you tell your waiter that carding you was further slowing down the flow of your meal service? *He probably would*, I thought. As I realized that it was turning into a power struggle with no clear resolution in sight, I removed myself from the situation by saying, "Just flag me down when you have it, and I'll be happy to check it for you."

Frustrated that his plan hadn't played out just how he expected, he brought out the big guns and began making his case against me. He listened closely as I took the orders of the other passengers around him. I moved on to the lady in seat 4A who appeared to have all the features of a sweet little grandmother. She was dressed in her finest and a bit heavy-handed on the blush. Anyone with a modicum of rationality could clearly tell that this woman was of an age far beyond the requirement to legally consume alcohol.

The little grandma in 4A asked for a gin and tonic, and I chose not to ask her for her ID because verifying her age would *actually* have been a waste of time. Well, not asking for her ID kicked off Mr. Big Shot's eruption of protest for the injustice that was taking place right before everyone's eyes. Mr. Big Shot, loudly, intending to make a scene demanded, "I want your name! I can't believe you! You're standing here badgering me to see my ID and you're not going to ask her for the same. That's age discrimination! I'll have you fired."

I was dumbfounded. I was following the rules. If someone appears to be under the age of 40, I am required to check identification. The same rules you would have expected to follow at a bar or restaurant also apply with serving alcohol in the air. I hadn't experienced anything like this yet in my career in-flight, so I stood there embarrassed and shocked without a plan of attack. I certainly have never had anyone threaten my job, and can you imagine that threat over something so silly?

I pretended to ignore him until I had finished taking the last two orders. The saving grace in that moment was that the other passengers in first class were scoffing at Mr. Big Shot as if he was a complete joke. He was obviously not 21, and his behavior was now the most telling sign.

Typically, anyone legally old enough to consume alcohol doesn't have a problem quickly flashing their identification because there is usually a mutual understanding that this is the law and the people checking IDs are just doing their jobs. Also, most people over the age of 21, myself included, are happy to be carded—it makes us momentarily feel young again, like we're being transported back to college. The good old days!

But the fact of the matter was that I didn't know how to handle this irate child. Was I the parent in the grocery store whose child was rolling around mid-aisle because I wouldn't let him have the cookies he wanted? I sure felt like it. I just wanted the ability to freeze time in that moment so that I could sneak out. I was rattled by how his lips never stopped moving and he wouldn't accept any reasonable justification I gave him for my actions thus far. I decided to avoid eye contact and beeline back to the galley.

I needed to call in the troops for reinforcement because I was floundering. Flustered, I told the Lead Flight Attendant about the situation. This woman was a middle-aged, seasoned flight attendant who was probably old enough to be Mr. Big Shot's mother. She agreed to talk to him and try to deescalate the situation. Before the Lead Flight Attendant stepped into the aisle, Mr. Big Shot decided he had been waiting long enough and it was necessary to ring his call light. The Lead Flight Attendant went out into the aisle to answer the call, and I could hear bits and pieces of their conversation. He seemed to be receptive to her reasoning for my actions, and his behavior seemed to mellow as his desire to speak to a manager had been satiated.

Still unsure whether this situation was diffused, I stepped into the flight deck to speak to the Captain. I wanted to make him aware of this situation because we were about to embark on a three-and-a-half-hour flight. The last thing we wanted was to deal with Mr. Big Shot's toddler tantrums the entire flight. Sometimes having the Captain speak to the passengers is enough for them to realize that the flight crew means business and childish behavior is unacceptable.

I filled the Captain in on all the conversations that had taken place, as well as the case that Mr. Big Shot was now building against me regarding my alleged "age discrimination." The Captain chimed in, "Yeah, it *is* age discrimination. That's exactly what it is, and that's exactly what you're supposed to be doing. That's how drinking laws work." Having no more time for this nonsense, the Captain excused himself and let me know that he would be back shortly. He walked off the plane and headed up the jet bridge.

What was his course of action going to be? Unsure, I went back to mixing and pouring the first-class drinks and attempted to deliver them to all the other passengers while strategically avoiding Mr. Big Shot, who was still talking off the Lead Flight Attendant's ear about how I wasn't capable of doing my job properly. I made it back to the galley, avoiding confrontation for a second time, where I waited for boarding to be complete. As I tidied up the galley and stowed the supplies I had used for the first-class drinks, I saw the Captain storming down the jet bridge with a piece of paper in his hand. He peeked his head into the galley where I was standing and said, "Feel free to watch."

The Captain stepped into first class and calmly approached Mr. Big Shot's row. "Sir, I hear you have some concerns regarding whether or not you should be served alcohol and whether or not age discrimination has taken place. Is that correct?" Mr. Big Shot, pleased that his concerns were being addressed by a man of authority, respectfully responded, "Yes, sir. That's correct. The flight attendant badgered me for my identification but didn't ask the lady sitting behind me for hers when she ordered an alcoholic beverage. I'm utterly embarrassed, and he should be reprimanded, if not fired, for his actions."

After listening to Mr. Big Shot's take on the scenario, the Captain empathized, "I can understand how you're feeling, sir, but we run things here just like any other establishment that serves alcohol in the United States. When someone appears to be under the age of 40, we check identification to be sure we're not serving alcohol to minors, an offense that could cost my flight attendants their jobs. This lovely lady behind you, while still young and beautiful, is undoubtedly over the age of 21." During an aside to the lady the Captain clarified that he meant no offense by assuming her age to be older than 21. She assured him that none was taken.

The Captain, returning to addressing Mr. Big Shot, justified my actions, "Asking for her ID would have been fu-
tile. But it seems that in your case, the request for
identification was the right choice." The Captain then read
Mr. Big Shot's first, middle, and last names aloud. "Do I
have the right person?" he asked.

The young boy confirmed that the Captain did have his
correct information—a signal to the Captain to continue.
"Perfect. I've got the right guy, then. Based off the information that you provided when making your flight reservation, you submitted a birthdate of May 17, 1999. That
means you just turned 19 years old last month."

Mr. Big Shot's eyes started to bulge, realizing that a
truth bomb had been dropped in his lap, and now he must
face the music for his attempt to complete an illegal act on
an airplane. I thought to myself, *I knew this punk wasn't 21
years old!* Hearing the Captain's fact check and learning that
I had been correct all along made me feel immediately vin-
dicated. Knowing that I had the Captain on my side, I
breathed easy watching the rest of the show comfortably
from my galley.

With the roles reversed and the Captain now having his
own concerns that he needed to voice to Mr. Big Shot, the
Captain continued, "With that said, I recognize that we all
have lessons to learn, so I'm going to give you a couple different options." The Captain transformed into a middle
school principal and everyone in first class perked up, waiting to hear what the punishment was going to be and how
he would turn this into a teachable moment.

The Captain then laid out Mr. Big Shot's potential consequences. "Your first option is to stop giving my flight attendants a hard time, behave yourself, and continue with us on this flight today—hopefully, you're heading somewhere fun for the weekend. The second option is calling authorities who will escort you off this aircraft and you can spend the afternoon answering their questions regarding why you're attempting to consume alcohol when you're under the legal drinking age. Which option do you prefer?" Realizing he really only had one option to choose, Mr. Big Shot slunk down in his seat and agreed to accept the first option.

The Captain verified that he made the correct choice. After confirming Mr. Big Shot's decision to behave properly, the Captain made a point to address the flight attendants loudly for all to hear, "And to my team, should you have any trouble with this young man, please let me know immediately. I don't tolerate that type of behavior on my aircraft and there will be significant consequences."

While I never imagined having to deal with this level of drama at the beginning of this flight, I was happy to see that the problem was resolved before we ever even left the gate. I began thinking about what the in-flight service would be like. I don't disagree that Mr. Big Shot got what he deserved, karma was alive and well, but now this whole experience had created even more awkwardness between us. I didn't want to deal with him the entire flight.

I knew that my working position included the responsibility of aiding the Lead Flight Attendant to be sure she quickly served her meals to all the first-class passengers. Then, once all meals had been served, I would help my colleagues in the main cabin finish their beverage service. This meant I would have to interact with Mr. Big Shot for at least the first 40 minutes of this flight.

Knowing how awkward the relationship between Mr. Big Shot and myself had become and how he would now be triggered by my sheer presence, I thought that the most professional thing would be to switch positions and work in the main cabin. The switch would allow me to avoid first class for the duration of the flight. I was sure that after his talking-to from Principal Captain he would have behaved just fine, but I didn't trust that he wouldn't try some convoluted trick or calculated revenge scheme to put me in my place — I pegged him for the type.

Attempting to avoid any of those potential hypotheticals, I explained the entire scenario to my colleague in the main cabin and asked her if she wouldn't mind swapping positions with me. She had no problem switching and completely understood my reasons for wanting out of first class.

The flight finally took off and each flight attendant completed their duties as normal. The cabin service was mostly completed when the colleague who switched positions with me came to the back to request a small favor. "Hey, would you please grab me one of those snack bags for purchase whenever you have a second?" she asked. I, of course, agreed to help her. She joked, "Your best friend up there is a picky eater." I was curious on the dirt, so I asked her what was going on. She was happy to indulge me. "Well, we had two options for meals, and he said that he didn't like either of them. What a shame, it's a nice grilled chicken salad for the cold meal and then beef tenderloin for the hot one. Whatever, more for me!"

I wasn't sure why, but I tried to rationalize his pickiness, "Maybe he has special dietary needs?" My colleague immediately shut the idea down, "Nope. I asked. Maybe he just doesn't have a very mature palette! I told him I'd get him the snack bag that has the Skittles in it. He seemed excited about it. I wasn't surprised, though. What *kid* doesn't like Skittles?!"

Did You Know

Flight attendants have separate bunk areas on the plane where they can rest while on break. In between services on transoceanic flights, we do get short nap breaks. Depending on the flight length, breaks can be anywhere from 1–4 hours long. On our larger planes, we have bunk areas with a small mattress pad, pillows and blankets and a little curtain that you can pull to darken your bunk. The crew rest area is essentially a room with a few sets of bunk beds. Each bunk is enclosed by walls on three sides, while one of the longer sides of the bunk has a curtain that spans the length of our bodies. The only downside is that they're not soundproof, so if Judy's having a hard time with her allergies, I need to be sure to have my ear plugs. Otherwise, good luck getting any sleep with all that snoring.

Zone Foreign Tongue

We all know there's only one reason someone goes to the airport: to people watch! Getting on a plane and flying somewhere is just the bonus. One afternoon, I landed in New York's John F. Kennedy International Airport, the Mecca for people watching. I had completed my pass through the customs and immigration hall, having just arrived from Rome, and I was ready to reenter the concourse to find the departure gate for my final flight segment home. With three hours before my flight, I had posted up to people-watch in one of the most diverse airports in the United States.

Whatever you're doing at JFK—waiting in line at security, walking to your departure gate, or grabbing your luggage in the baggage claim hall—you're sure to hear a variety of languages. This is one of the most beautiful things about my job. I've always been intrigued by languages and their complexities. Coworkers and passengers transition between English and other languages so seamlessly, and I've always found myself envious of this impressive skill. When I'm traveling, I do my best to take the time to learn the basics of a language; I feel I'm displaying respect for a culture by attempting to say my hellos, goodbyes, pleases, and thank-yous in the native language of the country I'm visiting. So, when I'm listening to others speak many different languages, I like to see if I can apply anything that I've learned.

With that said, my love for people-watching also includes people-listening. Usually if I hear a Romance language, I can piece together the meanings of phrases by referring to remnants of knowledge from my four years of high-school French class and being raised by my bilingual, Italian-speaking parents. Otherwise, I also consider body language to create the story that I think is being told in a language that I don't speak a lick of. For as many times as I've sat in an airport listening and watching, trying to decipher what other passengers are saying, today would be the first time I successfully decoded a language that I didn't understand.

The story began when I first stepped up to speak to the gate agent. Flying standby, a perk of the job, I wanted to make sure I would have a seat for my final leg home. Knowing an excursion to briefly chat with the gate agent would be a gamble resulting in the loss of my seat in the gate area—with both charging outlets and a view of the runway—I accepted the risk and unfortunately, another passenger swooped in and snatched my prime real estate. It's to be expected—it's the way Airport Musical Chairs works.

This round of the game landed me without a seat and I've never been more grateful to be displaced, because it led me to a seat next to a family of three. A father and mother sat with their son, who I'd venture to say was 12 or 13 years old. The parents were chatting quietly as their son absently swiped and tapped his way through a game on his phone. Additionally, three or four travelers were sitting near us, all wrapped up in their own personal pastimes, except one: New York Guy, or NYG for short. NYG was paying attention to what was about to ensue with the family, just like I was. There's nothing I enjoy more than having someone to share in the craziness happening around me. More on that spectator in a bit.

The boy, almost whining, looked up from his phone and innocently asked his parents when it would be time for all of them to board. The father responded in English by saying, "Soon, we go first!" and then continued speaking to the son in a different language. The father then directed whatever he'd say next to both his wife and his son. I couldn't decipher any of the words of the language he was speaking, and all I knew as fact from my eavesdropping was that the family would be boarding first.

"First" could have meant a couple different things. The first boarding group is always "pre-boarding" for those people that need extra time or assistance. Curiously, I wondered if the family had a reason to board early, or if when dad said "First," perhaps he was referring to the first-class cabin and they'd board when that group was called. I happened to look over at the boy's boarding pass, which he'd been flapping through the air and brushing against his leg, impatiently waiting for boarding to begin. I couldn't help but notice that his boarding pass stated, "Zone 4." If someone in the family had a disability or required extra time to board, then the zone printed on the ticket would be irrelevant, ultimately disregarded. I wondered if maybe the mom or dad needed some extra time to board. My curiosity was piqued, but I wasn't sure that I even had the energy or attention span to dig up any more info on this family's boarding plan, but why not continue observing?

The sweet-as-sugar, helpful gate agent announced that the passengers requiring extra time or assistance could take advantage of the pre-boarding zone. The family collectively stood up and headed quickly to the head of the line, meeting the gate agent. All three appeared to be in fine physical condition and have standard sized carry-ons — no obvious medical devices or oversized bags that would need attention or that would signal requiring more time than usual to board. The agent asked the family if they needed extra time boarding or if there were any extenuating circumstances that the flight crew should be aware of so that they could best assist throughout boarding and in flight. The three stood there, staring, not saying a word. They pretended they didn't understand anything that she was saying. They just kept trying to push their boarding passes toward the agent so she would scan them.

My jaw dropped as I sat there considering the level of scheming that took place just to board early. Rarely do extreme behaviors in airports or airplanes shock me, but today, I'll admit I was stunned. Well, now I had to keep up with the saga because we had a Tony-winning production right before our eyes. Who needs a Broadway play when there's a free performance at the JFK theater?

The agent deduced that none of the travelers had a disability, nor did they need extra time or assistance, but instead they had just run into a language barrier. She tried her best to tactfully slide them to the other side of the walkway with a guiding gesture. Here they waited in the general boarding lane, as she tried to convey that they needed to board with Zone 4. Kudos to her for trying to be consistent with the rules while also being gracious.

You may think, "Well, what's the big deal? It's three people—just let them get on." I'm sure plenty of agents pick their battles and sometimes they just let it slide. But all it takes is one passenger to write into the company regarding an observation of an inconsistency with company policy. Then, the employee must give a statement and has a "bad" letter in her file. I can understand why she was sticking to her guns.

While the mother and son slid out of the way, the father didn't budge. He moved his bags over ever so slightly while remaining an obstacle in the boarding lane for those that were granted access to board. His intentional protrusion into the boarding lane was an obvious second approach to receive permission to board, simply so he and his family would be out of the way. I watched as boarding passengers struggled to maneuver their bags around an inconsiderate traveler in their path; they had to lift their bags to avoid running over Dad's feet. Still, he stayed put.

Next, the gate agent called for the first-class passengers. Giving it a second go, the family of three attempted to board the aircraft again. Their boarding passes still read "Zone 4." The agent tried to explain again that they needed to move to the general boarding lane.

Recalling the family's conversation ten minutes prior to the start of boarding, I couldn't help but think that when the father chose to switch from English to a different language, it might have been somewhat calculated, like the way my parents would switch over to their Italian dialect so they could express themselves fully, i.e., cuss in a way that only their mother tongue allowed.

If I had to guess, I would have thought Dad said something along the lines of "Remember, you have to pretend we don't speak English. Understood?" Whatever he said must have been something that he didn't want the surrounding passengers to understand, so he chose to disguise it in a less commonly understood tongue. The response from the mother and son was completely memorable in that it was uttered firmly in unison with what I would have guessed was confirmation that they were both "all in" for the plan. I assumed that Dad wanted to board earlier because typically on full flights like this one, the passengers in later boarding zones, like Zone 4, are required to check their bags when overhead bin space is full. I could understand his frustration, and truthfully, I respected his game.

The idea of getting carry-on baggage stowed on the plane seemed to take a backseat to the now mortified mother and son who were dripping with embarrassment because Dad's genius plan wasn't working as he had imagined. While continuing to block the line for boarding and slowing the entire process, the family had become the center of attention when asked to move out of the way each time a new boarding group was called. This caused the son to dive face-first into his phone and the mother to avoid eye contact with anyone nearby—both with cowering postures that screamed, "Tell me when it's over!" After the second zone was called these two resorted to waiting in the general boarding lane, completely out of the way—they raised their white flag on the situation. The awkwardness was just too much for them to handle.

I caught a look from New York Guy—the lone traveler who I mentioned earlier. NYG is everything I imagined when I envisioned a caricature of an authentic New Yorker. He was dressed in a black puffy coat that appeared to be worn more for the purpose of warmth than for any trend of fashion, and he topped off his ensemble with a knitted tassel cap. Hearing his authoritative tone and distinctive New York accent, I knew he was a no-nonsense type of guy who would stand for none of this foolishness.

He said to me, "Are you seeing this garbage go down up there? That guy's pretending that he doesn't speak English and he's slowing down the whole boarding. Did you hear him tell his family to board first? He was speaking English just fine a minute ago. What's he trying to pull? Just to get on early?" He fired out his recount of the events so quickly and with such bold conviction that all I could do was nod my head in agreement. I agreed, not only to corroborate every detail of the story he pointed out, but also because I was enjoying listening to him continue in his disdainful New York-ian tongue. If I'm being honest, he could have just sat there screaming "Cawfee" over and over and I would have been engaged. All I could add that he hadn't already pointed out was, "Zone 4. They're in Zone...4!"

My boarding zone directly followed first class and as luck would have it, so did NYG's. We got in line, and predictably Dad tried to board the aircraft for the third unsuccessful time. At this point, all the agent could do was hold up a hand to the family, continuing to hold them back for yet another boarding group, as she thought this may be the only form of communication they would understand. Dad was becoming angry. His plan hadn't worked as he had thought it would, and there was no misinterpreting the agent's universal gesture for "stop, wait!" Spitefully, Dad refused to budge.

NYG and I approached the agent to have our boarding passes scanned. I was in front of NYG, and I awkwardly scooted my way around Dad. I stumbled a bit and shot Dad an I've-been-traveling-too-long-today-and-I'm-over-your-pettiness glare, as he continued blocking the boarding lane. Now it was NYG's turn to attempt to scoot around him. I tried to stay focused on scanning my boarding pass, but I couldn't help but focus on the interaction that had the potential to rank as *the* airport scene of all airport scenes. Shame I didn't stop at the newsstand to buy some popcorn beforehand.

With an unexpectedly friendly tone, NYG looked to Dad and asked, "Oh hey man, you wanna go ahead of me? Are we cutting in front of you?" Forgetting that he was mid-performance, Dad nonchalantly responded, "Nah, I've got to wait for Zone 4." The gate agent heard Dad respond in English and realized that she had been played.

NYG had her back, though. He reached the top volume I had originally expected moments ago, "Oh, so you *do* speak English? This whole time this nice, young lady has been trying to kindly ask you to wait for your zone and move over so you don't block the way, but you've got the balls to pretend you don't understand English just so you can walk on the plane before everyone else when you're in the last boarding group." Then, shifting to a firm and slightly threatening tone, NYG said, "Stop bothering this lady and move over to the other side so we can get the hell out of here on time. If I miss my connection because you're slowing down boarding, you're going to answer to me, and I'm not nearly as nice as this woman."

NYG: 1, Dad: 0. I really hoped for Dad's sake that there wouldn't be a Round 2. This was a match he had no chance of winning. Even though I was out of uniform, no adornments to tag me as a flight attendant, I refrained from getting involved with the situation. Having weighed my options, taking part in drama wasn't worth the risk of losing airline flight benefits. Offering my "Amen" in response to NYG's public testimony, I whispered, "Bloop!" to the agent who giggled in return. She was looking down and smiling, trying not to let anyone see that she also approved of the scolding Dad received after she had been bamboozled.

Prior to walking on the plane, I thanked her for the kindness that she had shown me and all the other passengers that day. Dad, embarrassed after being outed by NYG, finally moved himself and his belongings to the general boarding lane while NYG and I headed down the jetbridge. Heroes don't always wear capes, folks. Sometimes, they wear black puffy coats and knitted tassel caps.

TRAVEL TIP

Disinfecting wipes are a wonderful thing to pack in your carry-on. Give your seat, armrest, monitor, and tray table a brisk wipe-down to freshen up your area. You know that tray table you feel comfortable eating your snacks from? All I can think about is how the guy sitting in your seat on the last flight was piling his toenail clippings in the same spot where your crackers are laying. Of course, we discourage such actions on the airplane, but oftentimes we notice them after the damage has already been done. Don't forget your wipes!

Potato

One afternoon, I was working on a flight where we offered our normal beverage service and three snack options. My colleagues and I were serving the passengers, nothing out of the ordinary. Across from me on the cart was a flight attendant who had been working with the airline for over 30 years. Even after all those years of flying she showed up to work with a smile on her face and the patience of a saint. Having that trait makes for a very pleasant working environment and a smooth three days of flying together.

As we both continued smiling at our passengers, we were nearing the end of service with maybe 9 or 10 more rows of passengers to serve, so, between the two of us, that wouldn't take very long at all. I stepped up to a seat set of three passengers and I addressed the passenger at the window first. Sitting there was a gentleman dressed as if he was returning from a business meeting. He was wearing a crisp pair of khakis, a brightly colored plaid shirt with an unbuttoned collar and a deep navy blazer—the typical business casual attire.

This businessman seemed engrossed with the movie playing on his in-seat monitor. I thought I might have to wave my hand in front of his face or ask the person next to him to get his attention, but I was pleasantly surprised to see that he was more than ready when I approached him. He snatched his headphones off his head and grinned at me like a child. This must not have been his first rodeo. "Good afternoon, sir. May I get you something to drink?" Without pause he accepted, "Sure, Can I have a Coke Zero, please?"

I poured the businessman his Coke Zero, passed it off, and he thanked me for the beverage while simultaneously placing his headphones back on. He couldn't wait to get back to his movie—he must have been getting to the good part. My interactions continued with his two seatmates as I fulfilled their drink orders and then headed into snack territory. I listed the three options out to the seatmates who made their selections. The businessman finally noticed that I was passing out snacks and removed his headphones again to catch up with what he had missed. Speaking slowly because I hate repeating the options and I had already listed them just a moment ago, "Sir, today we have peanuts, pretzels, or cookies. May I get you something to munch on?" Without hesitation, loudly and clearly, he responded, "Potato!"

Did he just say, "Potato?" I'm pretty sure none of my options sounded anything like "potato." Let's try this again, I thought. "I apologize sir, I must have misunderstood you, but our options are peanuts, pretzels, or cookies. Which would you like?" Annoyed that he had to be interrupted to hear the options again after clearly stating his choice, he articulated with a slight bite, "I said, potato!"

Having cleared up the confusion, he went right back to watching his movie as if he had simply said "pretzels" and I was the idiot for not having already handed them to him. I was confused. This gentleman was speaking English very clearly, and I detected absolutely no accent at all, so a language barrier was off the table for explanations. I guess it was possible that maybe "potato" could have been short for something like "potato chips," but those were never an option either time that I listed the three snacks. I wasn't sure that repeating them for the third time would resolve the issue and I could also tell from his tone that he was not going to tolerate any more interruptions, so I better hurry up and figure out what kind of "potato" this guy was expecting.

If I'd had a potato, I would have handed it over. I'm a people pleaser in that way—I think almost every single flight attendant is to some extent. I want my passengers to be happy and if there is something that I can do to make them more comfortable or enhance their flying experiences, I am genuinely willing to do it. I had only been working as a flight attendant for a couple months when this happened, so I hadn't yet filled up my bag of tricks with strategies to handle strange situations like this one. After some reflection, I brainstormed options for the future, like holding up the snack options and letting him choose from what was in front of him or directing him to the menu in the seat pocket which had pictures of each of the options that we serve. Then, he could have, at least, pointed at his choice. But at the time, I just stood there and looked around like a lost child while trying to think of how I could get to a positive resolution to the problem that seemed to have no solution in sight.

The seasoned flight attendant on the other side of my cart recognized that lost look. She had caught on to what was happening with this passenger and read my facial expression to say, "I need backup, please!" By now she was fully aware of what was happening on my side of the cart and she could tell that I needed an intervention. She said, "Hey!" to get my attention and then flashed me a wink and a big grin that said, "Mama Bear's got this! Don't you worry." I was happy to pass the torch because I knew that I still had a lot to learn, so I might as well take a step back and observe from the sidelines.

She reached into the snack drawer and grabbed a pack of cookies. She smiled the warmest smile at the businessman as he happily took the pack of cookies from her hand, only half-glancing at the snack while at least one eye always remained fixated on his seat-back monitor. Then, not only did he not make a fuss, he opened his cookies and snacked on them as if she just handed him a sleeve of French fries, a bag of potato chips, or whatever other form of spud this guy thought he had requested. He graciously returned the smile to her and kept snacking.

I tried putting the pieces together. There was a puzzle here that I had to solve. A cookie was not the same thing as a potato. The word "cookie" and the word "potato" don't sound anything alike. What about the brand name of the cookie? Nope, the brand name of the cookies sounds nothing like potato either. I know they certainly aren't going to taste the same, and it's not like the cookie used potatoes as one of its ingredients. What kind of magic powers did this flight attendant have to know that he wanted a cookie from his request for a potato? Surely all her years of experience had taught her something that I had yet to learn. I gave up and I had to ask. "Hold on! I'm not making the connection. How did you know that he wanted a cookie when he just kept asking for a potato?"

She looked me square in the eyes with her big, beautiful smile and cleared up the confusion, "Baby, he had no idea what he wanted. You gotta know when to hold 'em and know when to fold 'em. Smile at him, give a cookie, and keep on rollin'." She unlocked the brake on the cart, and we did just that. We kept on rollin'.

Did You Know

When asking passengers in the exit row if they are able to help in the event of an emergency, flight attendants must receive a spoken answer from every passenger in the row. Why? Because we need to be sure that you speak English fluently and that we'll be able to communicate with you during an evacuation. The last thing we want is to scream directions to the passengers in the exit row and for them to answer back, "No English!"

My Angel

We all have a story to tell. Every single day of our lives we have new chapters to write. We wake up hoping that as we pen the next pages of our books, they will be filled with laughter and happiness, success and accomplishments, beauty and love. Realistically, not every day can have a chapter filled with all those wonderful things. Some days, it seems that the challenge is to find even a fraction of one of those ideas; they can all seem so foreign and out of reach. Those are the days we rely on each other. We lift each other up and shine light on the beauty that surrounds us. We will always find common ground with empathy.

I met the woman who would teach me that lesson as I stood at the boarding door, welcoming the guests onto the flight—my last working leg of the day. While I always tried to greet the passengers with a warm, genuine welcome, I found that my most authentic salutations occurred prior to—what we call in the industry—the "go-home" leg. As the passengers continued trickling onto the plane, I noticed a woman entering the doorway with her hair a bit disheveled and her eyes red and puffy. Her make-up was smudged and running; no doubt that she had been crying. Aside from these two notable features of her appearance, I wouldn't have suspected anything out of the ordinary with this passenger as she carried herself professionally and rolled her luggage on board just like any other traveler.

Being sure to offer her a notably kind smile, I greeted her, "Welcome aboard! How are you doing today?" No reply. I should mention that I never got the sense that her decision to withhold a reply was due to a lack of manners or a conscious choice to blatantly ignore me. I could see from her face that her heart held a deep sadness. She mustered a half-smile as a substitution for the words, "I'm surviving. Thank you for asking about my day, but if I respond honestly about how I am doing, I'll most likely open the flood-gates, giving you way more than you bargained for with your boarding door greeting." Of course, she never actually said those words, but in that moment, her face said everything, and those words couldn't have been clearer. She walked to her seat.

Something about the interaction felt unresolved. I had never met this woman in my life, and she wasn't a familiar face. I had never seen her before, I had never spoken with her before, and I had certainly never sat with her while she cried before, but today I felt like I should. I started thinking about her actions a bit more. Passengers constantly board flights while distracted. They're mid-phone calls, listening to music, focused on finding their seats, or they are pretending not to hear us just so they can be left alone. Regardless, these passengers walk on board and completely ignore a greeting that's specifically designed to add a personal touch to the flying experience.

This woman, despite her blatant distress, still took time to acknowledge me with what little strength she had left—that half-smile. I realized that she made an effort to connect with me on a basic human level. Not to say that the other passengers intentionally avoided this moment, but with other activities being the center of their universe, the opportunities for connection with others around them seemed to be missed. Not with my sad friend, though. Not only did she value my presence that day and respond with an attempted smile, but she also allowed me a small glimpse into her soul.

I wanted to do something to change her day, if even just to let her know that I was there for her. I knew in my heart that whatever was causing this woman such pain wasn't something that I was going to be able to fix for her over the course of the next hour and a half, but I'd surely do my best to try. Nowhere in my job description did it read "therapist," and nor did I feel qualified to offer any kind of advice, but that's one of the things that I love the most about being a flight attendant. The challenges each day are different and the ways in which we support passengers don't always involve delivering drinks and snacks. Our main goal is to get the passengers from Point A to Point B safely. Sometimes "safely" getting from one place to another doesn't just mean fastening a seatbelt for takeoff. Sometimes it means showing empathy to support mental wellbeing.

I knew I needed to check back in with this passenger, so I decided to pass my greeting responsibilities off to my colleague. I explained that I would be back in just a moment as I wanted to quickly check on a passenger. I headed into the cabin to find this woman who seemed so filled with grief. I found her tucked away in the window seat of her row, sitting quietly, and staring out the window.

By this point, many of the passengers were still in the jet bridge and had not boarded the airplane yet, allowing me a brief moment to sit down beside her. She looked at me and displayed the same half-smile as when she stepped onto the plane. I didn't say much, attempting to tread lightly, "Hi again. I'm sorry to bother you, but I couldn't help but notice that you seemed upset. Please don't feel pressured into sharing anything, but I just wanted you to know that if there is anything at all that I can do to make the next couple hours any easier on you, please don't hesitate to ask."

Tears started rolling down her face. The armor that she promised herself she would wear in public was breaking down. Words began stumbling off her trembling lips, revealing snippets of this tragic puzzle, "Going to Seattle . . . my mom . . . I left for a work trip . . . as soon as I got there my sister called . . . I didn't get to say goodbye." She wiped her tears away. I extended my hand, and she just held it for a moment. I told her how sorry I was that she lost her mother and that I couldn't imagine how hard it must be to take this flight home.

Based on her itinerary, I calculated that she was about to embark on a solid six hours of flying, and I couldn't fathom what it would be like to have that much time alone with my thoughts given the circumstances. She thanked me for listening and sitting with her. I assured her, again, that if she needed anything that I would be more than happy to get it for her. I also told her that she was welcome to join me in the galley to chat if she wanted to talk more about her mom or if she just wanted a distraction from her thoughts. Her tears continued as I stepped away with a heavy heart. I helped my colleagues finish buttoning up the cabin to prepare for departure.

The flight continued as normal with the flight attendants providing the beverage service. As I passed the distraught woman, I simply held up a "thumbs up" gesture and mouthed, "You doing okay?" to not draw any additional unwanted attention to her. She responded with a head nod and smile, then mouthed back, "Yeah, I'm good. Thanks." We finished the beverage service, took the carts back to the galley and restowed all the supplies of cups and coffee pots that we used.

I couldn't stop thinking about how sad this woman was at the loss of her mother, and what she must be thinking and feeling right now. What could I possibly say that would help her cope with the sadness that she was feeling? I continued to think of ways that I could support her without passing by every five minutes and asking if she was doing okay with an awkward thumbs up.

Lost in thought, I envisioned my family and how they showed up for each other in times of sadness, specifically around death and funerals. My big Italian family has always leaned on food — I'll admit we happily accept the stereotype of always being surrounded with too much to eat. We bake and cook in large quantities and deliver it to the person grieving. When dealing with all the decision-making surrounding a death and attempting to keep grief at bay, the last thing you want to do is worry about finding food. Honestly, who can even think about cooking or doing dishes when there are so many other responsibilities? Unfortunately, I had no ingredients or means to make this grieving woman a pan of lasagna, but the next best option was to collect some snack items from the galley that might provide her with some nourishment for the rest of her travels.

I pulled together a small package of snacks that I thought would be more substantial for the remainder of her travels: a banana, a couple granola bars, a few sweet treats, and a couple bottles of water to help her stay hydrated. I didn't have a nice gift bag for proper presentation, but I did remember that I had a blank greeting card in my bag.

Several months prior to this day, I had had a conversation with another flight attendant about how he kept blank greeting cards in his bag. He used them to send quick notes to family and friends while traveling, but he also mentioned that sometimes extenuating circumstances would arise with a passenger. Referring to the greeting cards, he said, "You never know when someone will need this most." This was one of those circumstances where I thought someone would definitely appreciate a card.

Fortunately, with the advancements in technology, I was able to add an extra note inside this card. I was able to figure out the exact flight that this woman would be taking to Seattle and reach out to the flight attendants on her next flight. As luck would have it, one of my classmates from flight attendant training was working the second leg of this woman's itinerary. I touched base with my classmate and gave her a heads up about my grieving passenger's story. I asked my classmate if she wouldn't mind checking in to make sure my passenger was comfortable on the longer leg of her journey home. My classmate was, of course, happy to help.

I grabbed the bag of snacks and made sure it was packaged to be easily tossed into a carry-on. I started brainstorming a message to write in the greeting card to avoid rambling, then began writing. I explained why I wanted her to have a bag of snacks, told her the location of her connecting flight's gate, and assured her that one of my good friends would be working her flight and watching over her on this last leg home. I told her that if she needed anything, she shouldn't be afraid to ask any of the flight attendants on the next crew, because they've been made aware of her story and they would be there to support her. I sealed the card and headed to deliver the care package of sorts. When I arrived at her row to drop off the package, I noticed that she was sound asleep with her head against the window, emotionally and physically exhausted. I asked the gentleman sitting next to her if he wouldn't mind lowering her tray table and setting the card and care package on the tray as a surprise for when she awoke. He happily obliged.

The flight was nearing its end, and we were pulling up to the gate to park at our destination. The passengers collected their personal belongings and the deplaning process began. My colleague and I thanked each of the passengers for flying with us as they disembarked. Then, seemingly out of nowhere, a set of arms was wrapped around me, squeezing me tightly. I immediately knew who those arms belonged to, and I returned the hug. Out of the corner of my eye I could see that she was holding the opened greeting card in her hand and I could tell that she was crying based on the trembles from her chest. She whispered in my ear, "My angel," before she released her grip from our embrace and offered another "thank you" to the collective staff. She walked away as we both wiped away our tears. I felt her gratitude in the strength of her embrace, and I learned in that moment how the smallest acts of kindness and empathy could feel like a manifestation of overwhelming support. From that day forward, I've always been sure to keep a couple greeting cards in my luggage.

FREQUENTLY ASKED QUESTIONS

Is this your regular route?

Very rarely do flight attendants fly the same routes on the reg. Not to say it wouldn't be possible for a flight attendant to fly between similar city pairings, but most of us don't expect it to be a frequent occurrence. In fact, most flight attendants find that their schedules will vary each month as they bid different layovers and rotations with the hopes that their seniority will hold the trips they desire. Unless, of course, you've been a flight attendant since the time of Wilbur and Orville Wright. In that case, Barb, Kathy, and Sheila will be your flight attendants to Sydney, Australia, every Tuesday.

Scent Sleuth

Working a flight home from Europe, the passengers had started boarding, finding their seats, and exploring the different amenities of the aircraft. Getting comfortable, each passenger mentally prepared to make our long journey back to the United States. With eight hours of travel ahead of us, even I had to give myself a pep talk before takeoff. That's the frustrating thing about working trips to Europe: No one ever wants to leave, and when you finally do have to leave, you have an extensive flight ahead of you, making the desire to stay even stronger.

Based on the first 10 minutes in flight, I wished I had stayed in Europe. Taking off, we barely reached cruising altitude when a call light illuminated. I hoped that someone just needed a new set of headphones or another blanket. As I got up from my jumpseat to locate where the call light was, one of my colleagues appeared in the galley already handling the situation, "Clean-up in Aisle 5!" I thought, *Al-*

ready? It's going to be that kind of flight? I asked her what was happening.

She was fumbling with the heavy-duty garbage bags, trying to separate one from the stash like you would at the self-check-out line of the grocery store when the bags are stuck together. "There's an old lady throwing up," she shared, then pointed out half-jokingly, "You're the most junior flight attendant on board, shouldn't you be cleaning this up?"

Triggered by the words "throwing up," I made a swift lap around the galley. Sanitary wipes? Check! Warm wet towels? Check! Dry Paper Towel? Check! I was equipped to head to the front lines. "I'll take care of it. I'm not a sympathetic puker, so I don't really mind."

Having finally separated the trash bags, my colleague happily handed them over, symbolizing her willingness to relinquish clean-up responsibilities while offering me good luck, "May the odds be ever in your favor!" I laughed, playfully snatching the trash bags out of her hand to complete my "clean-up kit" as I went to see how I could take care of my sick patient.

When I reached her seat, the elderly woman's forceful vomiting hadn't ceased. Her family was comforting her and she, thankfully, already acquired a sturdy bag, making clean-up much swifter. As the woman slowed her breathing and calmed herself, I offered her each component of my "clean-up kit" so the poor thing could refresh herself and start over. Flight home: Take Two! I chatted with the woman to see if she had any inkling of the illness' origin.

She couldn't pinpoint the cause, but she had a feeling that what she ate earlier that day may not have been sitting well with her.

Based on the smell that was lingering around this woman's row, I would definitely say something she ate wasn't agreeing with her. Sparing any further description of the pungent odor, it would suffice to say that the cabin's fragrance wasn't off to a great start. While I'm certainly not a medical professional and I had no true diagnosis of the situation, the only advice I could offer was to encourage her to wait for a bit before consuming anything else. The last thing we wanted was for Round 2!

Walking away from the older woman, I was stopped by a mom sitting with her husband and two younger children a few rows back. "I'm so sorry to bother you, sir. I know you're busy. There just seems to be a strong unpleasant smell. I was wondering if you had any kind of air freshener or spray that we could use that might help." Knowing that the family was sitting close to the older woman, I assumed the older woman's handiwork was the culprit for the pungent smell. I acknowledged her request, "Of course, miss! I should mention that I think I've addressed the root of the situation, so there should be a noticeable improvement shortly. I think that a spritz of air freshener certainly wouldn't hurt either, though, so I'll grab that for you in just a second." My response satisfied her request and to be sure she knew that I had followed through with my promise, I stood nearby as I lightly sprayed some of the air freshener.

Approximately 20 minutes went by. As I was walking in the same general area, I noticed that the smell had not gone away as I had expected it would. I had assumed that the vomiting incident was the source of the smell, but as time went on, I realized I was very wrong. I was so close to the older woman that perhaps the scent was still stuck in my nose. Now that the sick had been cleared away, a new smell had been introduced to my nostrils; this must have been the smell that I assume the mom had been experiencing from the start. A new call light illuminated, and it was the mother again. "I'm so sorry to bother you again. Do you think you could spray a little more of the air freshener? The smell is getting stronger, and it's very hard to ignore."

I promised the mother, again, that I would spray some more in just a second. She was appreciative that I would honor her request, and I was happy to, because she had been so pleasant and polite. Taking a step away from the family, I immediately stumbled upon another whiff of what Mom and her family had been smelling. The scent was undeniably body odor. I couldn't have been more wrong about the root of the smell. While grandma's upchuck didn't smell of roses and lavender fields, it definitely wasn't the odor that the family of four kept smelling.

Directly across the aisle from the family was a couple who I had noticed as they were taking their seats during the very end of the boarding process. Each of them had scrambled to find a location where their vibrantly colored, oversized backpacks could be stowed. The backpacks they lugged weren't bags that you'd see a teenager sling over one shoulder on the way to Algebra class; these backpacks were expensive totes, packed to the max with everything that two young folks would need to survive a trek across Europe for weeks, maybe months. I finally made the connection and was experiencing my "Aha!" moment. I identified the source of the odor that Mom continued pointing out.

Now that we knew the source of the problem, what was going to be the plan of action? Quite frankly, many of the crew members and I were stumped with how to handle this in the most respectful way. Obviously, the young couple had been traveling for a long period of time and we could assume that they hadn't stumbled upon an opportunity to take a proper shower or run their clothes through a laundering cycle. We certainly didn't want to embarrass them or call any more attention to the smell. What could we do? I decided to put Mom in charge of the air freshener bottle, holding her responsible for keeping their seat area smelling fresh. Other than that, we needed to be creative.

After meals had been served and cleaned up, passengers began winding down and snuggling into their seats. Seeing the exhaustion on the couple's faces, I wasn't surprised to see that they both had drifted off into a deep sleep, leaning on each other. Having some downtime, I took a minute to brainstorm a resolution. I remembered a flight attendant teaching me a trick to use whenever the lavatory wasn't smelling the freshest. She recommended taking an unused coffee pouch and placing it inside one of the hidden compartments of the lavatory. By having the pouch in there, it gave off a fragrant aroma of fresh coffee and it helped to mask any unpleasant smells that stuck around. I thought it through, *What if I placed a couple coffee bags in the general vicinity of the couple? Was it possible that it would help mask the smell? If I could do it discreetly, without others noticing, I might be able to address the smell without drawing any attention and without hurting the couple's feelings.*

Most of the passengers were sleeping or heavily engaged in their movies, so I thought that now would be the best time to execute my plan. But then, I had another idea. *What if I could use an unsuspecting accomplice?* Directly behind the couple sat a young boy, 8 or 9 years old. He was an unaccompanied minor, meaning that his parents or guardians arranged his travel and flight with the airline such that he would be traveling by himself and under the care of the flight attendants for the duration of the flight. A team member of the airline would escort him through every step of the journey. Being one of those team members, I had built a rapport with him.

I decided to ask him for his help. "Hey bud, how are you doing so far?" Removing his headphones to answer, "I'm good, Mr. Flight Attendant! Thanks! How are you?" I wanted to bottle his manners and share them with the world; he spoke eloquently and was wise beyond his years. He probably forgot my name, but I still thought it was cute that he was so respectful by calling me "Mr. Flight Attendant."

I leaned in, speaking quietly, "I'm great, but may I ask you a favor?" The seat next to him was open and my idea was to line the floor air vents with the coffee bags to circulate some of the coffee smell around the couple in front of him, "I have some air filters that I'm going to put by the floor vents next to you. Is it okay if I sneak by you very quickly to line them up?" The unaccompanied minor was very accommodating of my request. I thought that if I referred to the coffee bags as air filters, I could avoid questions about why I brought unused coffee-filled filters and why I wanted to lay them all over the floor. The strategy was good in theory.

With the coffee filters planted, I stepped away from my little friend when a call light rang again. I looked up and the light was above the elderly woman I assisted at the beginning of the flight. I stepped up a few rows and this poor woman was vomiting again. I ran to the galley to go through the motion of rebuilding another clean-up kit and then ran back to her seat. Luckily, she kept a garbage bag in her seatback pocket as a precaution after the first incident; for that I was eternally grateful! I went through the same waiting period for stabilizing the woman and I inquired about how she was feeling. She regretfully admitted her mistake, "I should have listened to you. I felt hungry and thought I was safe to finish the other half of the sandwich that I started before we took off. My stomach just isn't ready for food." *Told ya!*

Why was the universe continually punishing all of us with a variety of the worst smells today? Every time I resolved one issue and thought I had contributed to the comfort of all the passengers and crew members, another lovely aroma appeared. Walking away from the older woman, I was heading past the mother who continued playing the role of Classroom Mom for the back of the aircraft today.

She made sure to keep the area continually smelling good having taken charge of the air freshener. I gave her a thumbs up with a raised eyebrow, so I didn't have to interrupt her movie to check to see if the scents had lightened a bit. She pulled her earbuds out and whispered, "I'm good. It seems to smell quite a bit better—like coffee. It's not so bad anymore." Happy to hear that I didn't have another problem to solve and my plan was successful, I thanked the mother for being so understanding, patient and helpful. Then, I took a quick moment to chat with her about the movie she was watching.

Seeing that I was casually enjoying my conversation with the mother as I stood in the aisle, my unaccompanied minor took a moment to tap me and offer a bit of feedback of his own. But instead of using a regular indoor-type voice he brought his resonating playground voice. He hadn't realized he was speaking so loudly because he wasn't cognizant that his headphones stifled his hearing—a common occurrence on airplanes typically with the elderly and young children. He screamed, "Mr. Flight Attendant, these air filters are GREAT! They smell just like coffee, and I think I know why you put them there."

Oh no! I thought to myself. *Please don't say it, kid.* With pursed lips and his index fingers pointing and motioning to the seats in front of him where the couple slept peacefully he added, "I think it's time that someone has the talk with them about washing real good with soap and hot water under the armpits." The jig was up, and the kid had sold me out at full volume for everyone to hear.

I genuinely had good intentions for this solution, hoping that it would be a completely respectful one. I just wanted everyone to be more comfortable without anyone's feelings getting hurt. Luckily, the couple had passed out with headphones in their ears and neither stirred when the young man screamed out his approval of my coffee bag trick. I was so glad that they didn't wake. The mother, however, had been present for my little friend's whole announcement, so she and I locked eyes and neither of us could hold our laughter in any longer.

My intention had never been to make fun of the couple—the exact opposite really. That certainly wasn't where our laughter stemmed from. We all just wanted to help the situation, and I guess the unaccompanied minor felt that we should tackle it head on, loud and clear for all to hear. He just wanted to praise me for a successful solution and he also felt that a direct conversation was a mature fix for educating others. He wasn't wrong. To this day, I'm still trying to figure out if it was so funny because the young boy was so matter-of-fact, or if it was because I was so nervous at the idea being exposed that I couldn't help but laugh. Either way, we shared a humorous moment, we made it home safely, and no one's feelings were hurt.

That evening, as soon as I arrived home to my apartment, I took the longest, hottest shower and lit every candle I owned. I did everything in my power to be sure I didn't have to smell one more unpleasant scent for the rest of the day.

TRAVEL TIP

When traveling with young ones, where does your checklist of preparations end? Did I pack snacks? Did I pack toys and activities? What about medicines? Diapers? You've got so much to think about. I can help. Here's one thing you don't ever have to worry about packing for an airplane ride: Play-Doh. Electronic tablets are great. Coloring books and playing cards travel well. But leave the dough at home! You don't want to clean it up and I don't want to clean it up. The last thing I want to do is tell a businessman that he has crumbs of neon orange clay stuck to his ass when he's wearing a very expensive suit. I'm begging you to please leave the devil's clay at home.

Hidden Cameras

Who doesn't appreciate a compliment? I love that color on you! You have a beautiful smile! Those glasses are so fresh and unique! A simple phrase of praise to accompany a welcome can really make someone's day. While those type of compliments are wonderful to give and receive, can you think of anything more flattering than compliments as part of a scheme to acquire free alcohol? Yeah, neither can I. In fact, I don't think there's anything I look forward to more than a buzzed passenger laying it on thick in an attempt to acquire more alcohol.

We had boarded almost the entire plane of passengers, not needing the full allotted boarding time due to the smaller size of the aircraft, and we could tell from our devices that we were waiting on one more passenger, if he or she arrived in time. As we approached 10 minutes prior to the scheduled departure time, Mr. Fabulous, a man in his early- to mid-thirties stepped up to the boarding door. He was well-dressed from head to toe in designer clothing. He was dripping in signature prints, eye-catching patterns, and every logo known under the designer sun, instantly establishing that the phrase "less is more" wasn't one with which he was familiar. One look at this guy and I knew he was literally and figuratively going to be the most colorful passenger of the day.

He sashayed down the aisle as if it were his runway, stomping past every other traveler who was seated and settled, awaiting his arrival. Each one of these other travelers must have been an attendee of his fashion show, not possibly on that plane for any other reason than to see Mr. Fabulous strike his most couture poses at the location of this year's most innovative and breathtaking step-and-repeat, an altitude of 32,000 feet.

Where to look first? My eye was caught by his $9,000 handbag that was swinging back and forth and blinding everyone with the glare from the metallic studs and bright colors. Each time the angle of the bag caught a glimpse of the sun, the flash from the glare was a warning sign to the passengers that they must lean inward towards the window if they wanted their heads intact. Otherwise, they would simply become runway casualties, all in the name of fashion.

The eye rolls from passengers and crew members were aplenty. As crew members, we learn about many different cultures — gestures and body language, traditional clothing, and even customary scents and perfumes. So, quite frankly, airline workers are probably the most open-minded group of people that you will ever meet. We have grown accustomed to eccentric passengers and accept everyone on board without judgment based on their looks. While the passengers were probably rolling their eyes because of what seemed like a longing for attention from Mr. Fabulous, the flight attendants were rolling their eyes, in the privacy of the galley, for a completely different reason.

When Mr. Fabulous stepped onto the plane, he was greeted with a "Welcome aboard," just like the other 153 passengers prior to him. He removed his sunglasses from his face in what I assume was an attempt to appear more sincere and relatable. His garments and accessories aside, he was a very attractive man. Not quite tall enough or muscular enough to have the New York Fashion Week model-type build, but no one would deny that he was a handsome guy. Handsome *and* charming really—there was a certain *je ne sais quoi* about him. He could connect with and pull in an audience, making the lies that came out of his mouth seem convincingly plausible. Attempting to pull my colleague and me in, he improvised through all the talking points that would hopefully lead to achieving his ultimate objective.

With the tone of a sleazy salesman looking to hook a new client, Mr. Fabulous started in on those key talking points, "Hey guys! How's your day going so far? You doing okay?—Great! So glad! So yeah, I was just chatting with the gate agent and she was telling me that I should check in with the flight attendants whenever I got on board. I'm a frequent flyer with status and I wanted to buy a first-class seat for this flight. She said there might be one open, but that I would need to check with you guys first and we could take care of payment for the difference in seat prices once I was on the aircraft."

"I'm so sorry," I apologized, "but unfortunately we don't have any seats in first class available at this time." Mr. Fabulous pushed further looking for an exception, "So, there wouldn't be a way to just buy someone out of their seat?" Sort of stunned by this idea, I confirmed that we couldn't do that while simultaneously I thought, *For real? Who the hell asks if they can buy someone out of a seat on an airplane?!* Just to be sure we recognized how serious he was, he was sure to tell us that we needed to let him know first if that option, or a first-class seat, became available. "Sure thing," I said.

And this is when the crew's collective eye rolls came into play. I applaud Mr. Fabulous for his valiant efforts but the outline below clearly explains all his rookie mistakes. We've heard it all before, sir.

First off, flight attendants don't deal with payments of seats—Beer? Yes! Vodka? Yes! Seats? No! We have no way to ring up an upgrade on those nifty little devices and nor do we want that responsibility. We're happy to leave those upgrades to the gate agents. So you might hear us say, "If you'd like, sir, we still have ten minutes left before departure if you'd like to speak with the gate agent about purchasing an upgrade to a different seat."

Secondly, the gate agent has full authority over seats when we are still at the gate and boarding hasn't completed. Rarely will a flight attendant ever move another passenger from their assigned seat before the boarding door is closed.

Should a passenger show up who was originally assigned to a seat, then the flight attendant has created a "dupe," or two people assigned to the same seat. That can be very upsetting to the passengers and a huge, unnecessary headache to the crew.

And finally, every single seat on the plane was occupied except for the last remaining seat that Mr. Fabulous was assigned. Had he actually approached a gate agent and inquired about a seat in the first class cabin or an upgrade based on his status, she would have informed him that every seat was taken and all passengers in first class had checked in and boarded. He would have known that asking a flight attendant for an upgrade would be a waste of his time.

The plane capacity spoke for itself. We were full and there was no chance that Mr. Fabulous was purchasing an upgrade. Realizing this, he nestled into his seat after stowing both of his bags into the overhead bin, a traveling faux pas that none of the flight attendants felt was worth addressing because he was the last passenger on the plane. If he was able to find room for both, and it got him seated quicker, we were all for it!

We finally took off and began the beverage service where Mr. Fabulous was ready to be wined and dined. I approached the row he was sitting in and asked if I may get him a beverage. He gave his lunch order, "I'll take two vodka-cranberries and one of the cheese assortments."

"I apologize, sir, but the cheese assortment isn't available on this flight. The availability of those items is based on the length of time of the flight and unfortunately the flight time falls just a bit short," I explained. He responded as if I had told him his Louis was fake: shocked and appalled. "Really? This flight already feels like forever. You don't have anything up there that's more substantial than the snacks on the cart?" I assured him that I didn't have any items for sale but that he could have as many complimentary snacks as he'd like if that would help satiate his hunger. With disappointment he agreed, "Well, I'll take two of everything that you have. I'm starving and I thought I would be able to, at least, buy a sandwich or something on this long flight."

That "long" flight was one hour and thirty-five minutes. Either way, giving him a few extra snacks wasn't going to hurt anything. We had plenty on board, and since he was drinking, I was willing to offer extra carbs to soak up the alcohol. You never know how a passenger is going to react to booze, and he wasn't shy about starting out with a double.

Mr. Fabulous seemed to be enjoying his snacks and cocktails. As the flight attendants passed through the cabin, he asked if he could have another vodka-cranberry. A refill would bring his vodka count to three mini bottles. Alcohol affects everyone differently, especially at a high altitude. While he seemed to be in the gleeful pre-intoxicated stage, he didn't seem to exhibit any actions that would lead me to believe he was already intoxicated. Therefore, cutting him off wouldn't have been an appropriate response.

So, I brought him the third vodka-cranberry and collected some of the empty wrappers from the snacks that he had devoured already. I made a mental note in my head to share with my crew that he had been given three vodka minis within a thirty-minute period.

While my colleague was passing through the aisle to collect trash, Mr. Fabulous caught her attention. Stopping her in her tracks, he asked if he could have another cocktail. She didn't think he appeared to be intoxicated. He seemed to be enjoying the company of his seatmate at only a slightly louder decibel than most other passengers, but aside from that he seemed pleasant. She made the drink and headed out to the aisle to serve him what he requested.

Looking into the aisle, I noticed that she was dropping off his drink, so I made it a point to share with her and the rest of my crew that the drink she just handed him was his fourth drink in less than 40 minutes. Some of our passengers are champion drinkers when it comes to holding their liquor, but on a flight that is 95 minutes long, the pace at which this passenger was going would have likely laid the plans for an alcohol-induced vomiting session all over his Gucci shoes.

Checking on passengers and wanting to feel out the situation for myself, I walked through the aisle to hand out glasses of water. I noticed that Mr. Fabulous' volume had increased drastically. Passengers around him were becoming irritated, and his poor seatmate was giving every polite signal in the book to let him know that she didn't want to converse with him any longer. Hoping to give her some reprieve and contribute to diluting the alcohol in his system, I offered glasses of water to both he and his seatmate, but no takers. I even attempted to encourage him to stay hydrated on "long flights" like these, because flying could really dry him out and it would be great for his skin. To my dismay, I couldn't get him to even let me leave one just in case he decided he wanted it later.

But I'll give you one guess at what he wanted instead of water. Mr. Fabulous declined the water and then shared, "I'm good, but I'll take another vodka-cranberry when you have a chance." All eyes turned to me. Everyone around him had already had enough of his behavior. He was initiating conversation with people who had politely declined several times, he loudly slurred his words, and his language was more colorful than his entire ensemble.

"Sir," I said, "at this time we're going to hold off from serving more alcohol. You've had quite a bit in a short amount of time. We have to slow you down — it's our policy, and more importantly for your safety." I had to put my foot down.

"I could just do one more and that would be good for me," Mr. Fabulous persuaded. He wasn't making this "cut off" process easy. I apologized again and tried to explain that I wasn't permitted to serve that many drinks to one passenger in such a short time frame. I offered coffee, soda, and pretty much anything else I had thought of that didn't include alcohol. He finally agreed to plain cranberry juice.

I grabbed his juice and I brought it out, laying it on his tray table. A gentleman behind Mr. Fabulous waved to get my attention to ask me if I just provided Mr. Fabulous with more alcohol. I had to explain that Mr. Fabulous wouldn't be receiving any more alcohol and that I had given him juice only. He was happy to hear that information because his frustration level was hitting a breaking point. That comment confirmed that other passengers had been bothered on their flight and certainly didn't have a good taste in their mouths regarding their overall flying experience.

I walked away, annoyed at the whole situation and wishing that the flight would come to an end. I felt like I was back in college with that one friend who wanted to start the night out with shots and then became the person that everyone ended up babysitting. Rather than enjoying your night out with friends, you end up walking around apologizing to everyone he encountered and hoped that sooner rather than later he'd just pass out and could be put to bed.

I would only have been so lucky to have looked out into the aisle to see Mr. Fabulous catching some shuteye. No such luck. Two of my colleagues were in the rear of the plane tending to that galley and taking advantage of some downtime before we landed, while an additional colleague and I held down the operation in the front galley. As my colleague in the front galley decided to head into the aisle to walk through and collect any trash items that had accumulated, Mr. Fabulous decided to get up from his seat and head to the front of the plane to use the lavatory. He maintained enough posture to edge his way up to the forward lavatory, stumble into it, and take care of business.

After finishing up in the lavatory and obviously skipping a handwashing, he stepped into the galley where I currently stood desperately hoping it was time for the initial descent. This particular front galley was split in half by the aisle that spanned the length of the plane. Spacious would not be a word that I would use to describe the amount of space in either half of the galley. In fact, no more than one person should have been standing on either side of the galley. It was cramped quarters and a recipe for spills and accidents when too many people were present. I was standing on the left side of the galley and Mr. Fabulous took a step in toward me and seductively whispered, "You . . . are . . . so . . . cute!" Not knowing how to respond, I tried to keep it polite and professional. "Thank you. That's very kind of you to say."

He moved in another step closer. *Oh shit,* I thought. By that point, my back was up against the aircraft door and I had nowhere else to go to avoid him. I began thinking of the least invasive ways to get him to respect my space. My mind wandered all the way to grabbing a coffee pot and bopping him with it. Having a plan, just in case, is always a good idea, but any kind of violent act should always be the last resort—at least, that's what I kept reminding myself.

As I was literally backed into a corner, Mr. Fabulous continued his gross whispers looking for a green light, "Let me kiss you!" Attempting to maintain my combination of politeness and professionalism I declined with a simple, "No, thank you!"

He wasn't giving up that easily. "Why not? You don't think I'm cute?" he asked, attempting to fish for an iota of interest that he could grasp onto.

"I think ... you're feeling brave from your drinks," I responded as I'm sure I was visibly uncomfortable being stuck against the aircraft's door.

Easing up a bit, he offered, "Aw, am I making you uncomfortable? Don't be! I'm not trying to!" Strangely enough, in his drunken moment, I could tell that he had realized that his proximity was making me quite uncomfortable and he gave somewhat of a narrow berth for escape.

Taking a slight step away, but still pursuing his goal he flirted, "I just think you're really cute and wanted to tell you that I wanted to kiss you as soon as I first stepped onto the plane."

Trying to accept his compliments without being dismissive, I quickly declined, "Again, that's really flattering, but I can't." Reaching my breaking point, I thought, *I bet you're the guy at the bar that can't take a hint and just keeps pushing until someone pours a drink on your head. Don't think I won't whack you with a wine bottle; it's been done before.*

"Just let me kiss you," he pleaded.

I snapped back firmly, "Hard NO. I'm working, and this is inappropriate."

Hearing the word "inappropriate" seemed to register with him. He took a step back and looked around. He eyed up a metallic circular knob directly above my head and vocalized his thoughts. "Oh! Right! You can't get caught on camera kissing me. They probably frown upon that, huh?"

Well, if you're gonna give me an out, I'm gonna to take it, I reasoned. "Yes, I would get fired for sure," I said confirming his hunch.

He stared at a small, silvery valve that was located directly above my head. It was round, metallic, and somewhat formal, allowing movement that spanned 360 degrees. I had an idea that was either going to set me free or was going to fail miserably. Realizing who I was dealing with and his current state of intoxication, I took my chances. I played my best round of charades, pretending to use my hands to snap an imaginary photo of Mr. In-My-Face-Vodka-Breath. Then, I pointed up to the knob to signal that pictures and video were recorded from the camera in the valve.

Thinking he had a genius solution, he proposed, "What if I just cover that camera? Nobody will know!"

Pretending to care about his idiotic solution, I dramatically shut it down, "That would be bad. *Really, really* bad — probably the worst thing you could ever do in the air. It would immediately set off an alarm to the pilots. Then, it would flag our operation center to tune into the live stream of that camera and all the rest to be sure everyone was safe, and you weren't a terrorist or anything."

Startled at the possible consequences, Mr. Fabulous backstepped, "Oh geez! Yeah, let's not do that."

Having had enough, I profited from his fear of the cameras and suggested, "I think it would be a great idea if you go back to your seat now. I don't want your actions to be misconstrued. We want to get you to your destination safely with no trouble!"

"Okay," he started and transitioned to a whiny beg, "but can I please just get one more vodka? I'll be good, I promise."

I explained that the same policy still applied and apologized, "I'm sorry, I just can't. If I could, I would. The seat belt sign has been illuminated, now, though. You need to take your seat quickly, my friend." He did.

Finally feeling free after being pinned in the corner of the galley, I grabbed the attention of the flight attendant who had left to pick up trash. I celebrated with her that I was able to get him to return to his seat and leave me alone without having to bash him with a coffee pot or a wine bottle. While I could have yelled at him or threatened to have the authorities meet the flight, there was always a chance that a seemingly friendly drunk would become belligerent and aggressive. Therefore, I was happy to try to resolve the issue in a way that left this passenger with an ounce of dignity, even if that's all that he actually had left. Then, I walked through the scenario as I explained to my colleague how he came onto me and how I got him to leave me alone.

My colleague giggled to herself, "Surveillance camera, huh?"

By that point, I was laughing with her, "Yep, that camera right there! You got it. I knew it might be risky, but I read my audience and I figured it was a risk I was willing to take."

Like a mother making sure I put a borrowed item back where I found it, she demanded, "Well, before we sit down for landing, make sure you redirect that camera so it goes back to pointing right at me. You know us old women, always having our hot flashes — we need those cold air vents blowing on our faces any chance we can get."

Did You Know

Overhead bin space is shared bin space. I've seen many passengers frustrated because the bin space above their seats was full upon arrival. Because the bin space is shared, you don't necessarily have to place your items directly over your seat set. Let's do some quick math to explain why.

Typically, one overhead bin spans the length of two rows of seats. So, if we only look at one side of the aircraft, we could assume that one overhead bin is allotted for the six seats in those two rows. That one bin that is directly above those six seats only holds, at most, four large roll-aboard bags. If all six passengers bring a roll-aboard bag, at least two of the passengers are going to have to find a spot elsewhere for their bags.

So, before you go cussing out the flight attendant or telling off your fellow passengers because there's no space left, remember that you can place your bag in any available bin within your cabin of service. If your bag is stowed a couple of rows in front of you, I wouldn't worry about it going missing. It's not going to just walk off the plane midflight.

Brand Loyalty

Boarding a flight, passengers filed on, beginning with the first-class cabin, as usual. After a large chunk of these passengers were comfortably seated, the Lead Flight Attendant went out into the aisle to ask all the first-class passengers if they would care to have beverages before we departed from the gate. To make the service easier and less disruptive to the boarding process, the lead flight attendant went out into the aisle and collected all the orders at once. She brought back a list of the drinks that needed to be made, I poured them, and then she delivered them all at once.

Following through with that plan, the Lead Flight Attendant came back with the list, and as I was manning the bar cart, I began popping soda cans and twisting liquor bottles open. I had glasses of white wine poured, beer head settling, and sodas ready to be handed off. With two more drinks to make — both mixing vodka, soda water and a twist of lime, I thought, *No sweat!* I poured a miniature bottle of vodka into each cup, topped them each off with soda water, and added in a slice of lime. I lined up the drinks, and they were ready for delivery. My Lead Flight Attendant headed back into the aisle and passed off the beverages to their respective owners. We were done serving drinks on the ground, and we checked that responsibility off our list as boarding continued.

Prior to takeoff, the flight attendants were required to collect all the beverages that they had served on the ground as a regulation established by the Federal Aviation Administration. The lead flight attendant passed through the cabin and the passengers showed appreciation to her for cleaning up their empty cups. No complaints so far! Seemed like this flight was going just fine and all the passengers in first class enjoyed the first course of many onboard service components.

Once in the air, the lead flight attendant stepped into the aisle to take first-class meal orders. Upon returning she suggested, "Why don't you take drink orders and fill those, and I'll take care of laying linens and keeping an eye on the food." The plan sounded good to me.

I dove into the aisle and made my way, row by row, collecting and filling beverage orders. As I arrived at row 3, I expected that they were going to order vodka-soda-lime, just like they had ordered before we departed. Many passengers stick with the same drink throughout their entire flight experience, and quite often when someone starts with vodka and soda water, that will typically be what they drink for the duration of the flight. I remembered that 3C and 3D were both drinking the vodka-soda-limes because they were the last two drinks that I made. For some reason, their order had stuck in my head, so I expected to already know what their drink orders would be.

I greeted the passengers and asked them what I could get them to accompany their meals. The Gentleman in 3D was perusing the menu and then looked up to say, "I think I'll stick with my Tito's and soda, with a twist of lime." The Lady in 3C was quick to respond, "I'll have the same."

Realizing I didn't have the specific vodka requested, I hoped to find a suitable substitution, "Oh, I'm sorry folks, we don't carry Tito's on the plane. But I do have the vodka that is listed at the top of the menu you're holding sir. Our vodka is Smirnoff." The Gentleman in 3D cocked his head to the side and said, "What do you mean you don't have Tito's?" I thought my response was pretty clear, but I tried to be clearer, "We don't have that brand of vodka on the plane. Not that we're out of it, we just only offer Smirnoff vodka on our domestic flights."

I could see the Gentleman started to boil, "Well, I know you're lying because we drank Tito's in our drinks that we had on the ground. The lead flight attendant brought them to us." I hated being the bearer of bad news but that's fake news. I gently revealed the facts, "Sir, unfortunately, you didn't drink Tito's vodka on the ground. You drank Smirnoff vodka, mixed with soda water and lime. I'm sorry for the confusion, but the vodka was not Tito's."

Still not trusting my explanation, he continued, "I can tell when I'm drinking Tito's and when it's something else.

That was definitely Tito's, so I don't understand why you're choosing to withhold it from us." Annoyed at this ridiculous banter I reasoned, "Sir, I'm certainly not trying to upset you, nor am I withholding Tito's from you. If I had it, I would be more than happy to mix it into your drinks. What I think—"

I caught myself. I took a moment to decide if explaining to him what I thought had happened in this situation would even be worth it, or if finding out the truth would just upset him more. I knew exactly what happened before I even confirmed it with the lead flight attendant. Many times, when passengers order drinks, they order the type of alcohol they want using a brand name. For example, this couple chose to order Tito's and soda; Tito's being a specific brand of vodka. Sometimes, as in this case, the passengers will be passionate about the specific brands of alcohol they receive. I have had passengers who found out that we didn't carry the brands of alcohol that they enjoy, so they changed their drink orders all together. Perhaps they liked our brand of gin instead of our brand of vodka, so they would switch their original order of a vodka drink to a gin drink. This doesn't happen every day, but often enough that I'd never be genuinely surprised to see it.

In this case, the lead flight attendant heard the couple had ordered Tito's and recognized that this was a specific brand of vodka. So, what did she write down on the list of drinks to make? She had written "VSL," or vodka-soda-lime, for both passengers. She hadn't confirmed with the passengers that Smirnoff vodka would be served in place of Tito's, she simply wrote down "VSL." In her defense, I didn't think she was intentionally disregarding the request for a specific brand of vodka. Attention to detail wasn't her strong suit.

The Lead Flight Attendant obviously hadn't realized that the couple was so particular about their vodka choice. The chart with the orders got back to the galley and was laid in front of me. I had not been privy to any portion of the request for Tito's vodka, so I mixed Smirnoff vodka, soda water, and added lime. The drinks were passed off to the passengers, and they were happily sipping away on what they had thought was their "Tito's and soda."

The time had come to decide whether I would attempt to explain all of that to this couple or allow the lead to do the honors. The gentleman in 3D started to get worked up, and he had already called me a liar so by that point I had recognized this as an irrational interaction. I explained to the couple that I'd ask the Lead Flight Attendant to head out to speak with them so that she could sort out exactly what had happened with their drinks, and we could get them something that they would enjoy. They agreed that this was a good idea.

I briefed the Lead Flight Attendant and explained how the situation escalated. After I caught her up to speed with all the details, she told me not to worry about it, because she would take care of it. I thought, *Perfect! Have at it! They're all yours!*

The Lead Flight Attendant went out into the aisle, and I stood at the beverage cart, mixing other drinks as I observed the interaction between the Lead Flight Attendant and the passengers in row 3. Approaching the stubborn couple, she asked what she could offer them to drink.

"We were wanting Tito's and soda with lime, like the ones we had on the ground," he requested. Still avoiding the issue at hand, the Lead Flight Attendant repeated their order, "Okay, no problem. You want vodka-sodas with lime. We can do that!"

The gentleman in 3D wasn't going to allow her to pull the wool over his eyes this time. "Yes, but we want our vodka to be Tito's. We don't want Smirnoff vodka," he specified. In a sweet, apologetic voice the Lead Flight Attendant explained, "I'm sorry, Baby. We only have Smirnoff vodka. I didn't realize you wanted that specific type of vodka so when I had my colleague make the drinks, I just told him vodka, soda, lime, and he used the vodka that we have in our carts. That's my fault, I apologize."

There's something about an older woman calling you "baby" that takes away the rage over not getting your first choice of vodkas on an airplane. The Lead Flight Attendant continued, "You like what you like, right?! I respect that. May I bring you one out using the vodka we have and if you don't like it, we'll get you something you might like better?" The Gentleman in 3D hesitantly responded, "Sure, that sounds reasonable, I guess."

I thought about that response, *Oh, okay, now we're all just reasonable people bringing rational reasoning to the table?!* There was nothing reasonable about this solution. Had either of the guests called upon us on the ground to say, "Hey, we tasted these drinks, and these don't taste like you used Tito's vodka. We think this is some other type and we don't care for it," then, this would have been a different story. I would have trusted that they were connoisseurs of vodka and I would have appreciated that they didn't want the vodka that we offered. But that never happened.

Regardless, the Lead Flight Attendant found a way to bring an empathetic element to the interaction. She had apologized for not taking note of the specific brand of vodka and had given them the option to try the new drinks with a chance to swap for something they might like better if they didn't care for them. I appreciate how she handled it, but I still had a couple of questions. I thought, *Why would I withhold a brand of vodka from paying passengers, and why, after you became aware that the vodka wasn't Tito's, are you forcing us to participate in this game where we watch you taste a new drink that we both know damn well is going to taste exactly like it did on the ground?*

I didn't dare ask those questions, but instead, simply tried to get to a solution that made the passengers happy so we could all move on with our day. So, I played along mixing up two drinks the exact same way that I mixed them while we were on the ground. I put on my smile, and I walked into the aisle to deliver the drinks to the passengers. "All right, my friends, I have those drinks for you. Let me know what you think. Just like the lead said, if you don't like them, you let us know right away and we'd be happy to get you something else off the menu," I said laying the drinks down on their tray tables.

The two took sips of their drinks and looked at each other. The gentleman was the first to speak, "I just don't . . . want it. I'd rather have something else." Mimicking as she did so well the lady added, "Yeah. I agree. I'll have something else, too." I took a quiet deep breath to help in processing the level of absurdity that we had reached with this whole charade.

I felt like I was dealing with toddlers. This situation wasn't unlike a time that I took my three-year-old niece out to a restaurant for dinner. The kid was so excited for her favorite meal of macaroni and cheese and then when it came out with breadcrumbs and a sprinkle of parsley on top, she wouldn't touch it. The dish probably tasted just like the one she was used to, if not better, but with the added presentation of the garnishes she refused to try it. The cheesy pasta didn't look like the fluorescent-orange, boxed kind that she was used to eating at home, so she wasn't touching it.

Catering to my picky drinkers, I assured them it was no problem and that I wanted them to enjoy what they were drinking. I then asked them what they thought they'd like to have instead. The gentleman said firmly, "I'm going to have the light domestic beer," and following suit, as usual, the lady said, "I'll have a light beer, as well." By the way, I wasn't convinced that she even had a brain of her own. Her responses sounded as if a mechanism was installed that would replicate the last thing heard, then an additional word or two of agreement.

I grabbed the beers, still thinking this whole interaction was a joke, but I maintained professionalism and decided to ask some questions as an opportunity to get to know the couple better. "Okay, here are those beers. So, I was thinking, if you put a cup of Coke and a cup of Pepsi in front of me and ask me to identify which is which just by tasting them, I think I would be able to tell the difference. I can describe one as being sweeter than the other and if I were alternating sips of them right now, I might be able to give maybe one or two other descriptors of their differences. I've never been good at differentiating alcohol, though. I'm just curious, if you don't mind me asking: What differences are you able to taste in the different brands of vodkas?"

I'm not sure why, but I fully expected him to give me a response that compared the drinkability of one type over another in relation to its smoothness. Then, I thought maybe he would tell me that one had a more defined pungent flavor whereas another might be more easily masked when added to a mixer. He answered my inquiry, "We just think Tito's tastes better, in general. I don't know what it is about the taste, but it's just better. We just like to support American-made things. We like that Tito's is made here in the United States, in my hometown of Texas." Then, brilliantly, the lady in 3C added. "Yeah. We'd rather support businesses that are based here in the States, rather than drink vodka like Smirnoff that's based in China."

There it was: the reason why she probably only ever agreed with what he had said and didn't work too hard to contribute any original thoughts. I was at a loss for words, so I simply nodded my head and said, "I understand."

Leaving behind that nugget of brilliance, I resumed my flight attendant responsibilities. I respected their decisions to remain brand loyal to the companies of their choice, but if this was a matter of principle rather than a matter of taste, why did you ask me to make another round for tasting? Then, I remembered that these were the same people who had thought Smirnoff was a Chinese company, and suddenly the whole scenario seemed justified.

FREQUENTLY ASKED QUESTIONS

What did we just fly over?

Most major airlines have a flight path available to follow on the in-seat monitors as your flight progresses. More than likely, the flight attendants have been serving drinks and snacks or have been tending to other passengers' requests. Therefore, we don't have the slightest clue where we are, let alone what we just flew over. But it's flattering that you think we're that talented. If we had the mental capacity to identify our current position on the Earth at any given moment, we would be crafting software, not soft drinks.

Still Not Minnesota

As flight attendants, we're passing through different airports constantly, sometimes multiple airports per day. Just like our passengers, we need pick-me-ups in between legs of flying. Maybe it's a chocolate bar, a caramel macchiato, or a bag of chips—any treat can serve as that little "carrot" to dangle in front of ourselves to keep us motivated. But don't worry, the irony isn't lost on me that a carrot would be the last thing I'd choose as motivation for my day.

Because flight attendants are constantly looking for those motivational snacks, we become experts on our most frequently visited airports, so it's no surprise that we've nailed down all the "airport superlatives" like:

- the place with the healthiest and most substantial foods

- the place with the most authentic local fare

- the place with the widest variety of snacks

- the place with the best deal on a hot breakfast, and most importantly,

- the place with the fastest cup of coffee

Coffee: It's the most important meal of the day! By the way, "Were you able to have a cup of coffee yet today?" is a great leading question to ask a flight attendant, especially on an early morning flight. If the answer is "no" or some version of a mumble and grunt, please don't take it personally and go ahead and proceed in silence. I'm joking, you can talk to us — quietly please. Relying on coffee regularly, we've become professional coffee fiends. We will always be able to tell you where the closest, best tasting, or fastest cup of coffee can be found in the airport; your own personal coffee concierge at no additional cost.

While flying one day, I was passing through DTW in Detroit, Michigan, an airport I know like I know the back of my hand. As soon as we deplaned, I bee-lined to my favorite coffee shop for my usual quick cup of joe. Since I was between flights, I was in my full flight attendant's uniform, and if you weren't aware, wearing a uniform is synonymous with wearing a sign that says, "Please talk to me! Small talk satisfies my soul!"

I stepped into line, and I practiced my order in my head — Maybe it's because I'm always in a hurry, but I like to be prepared with my drink order once I reach the front of the line. We're all standing in line for the same thing, right? No one wants to be the asshat who snakes through the entire queue, waiting upwards of 15 minutes, and still approaches the cashier caught off guard that it's decision-making time. I refused to be that patron, so I had my order on repeat in my head. But that day, no matter how many times I practiced my order, the line wasn't moving any faster. With the extra downtime, the gentleman in front of me had the opportunity to turn around, get a look at my uniform, and strike up a conversation.

"So, where are you based?" he asked.

"Oh, I fly out of Minneapolis," I answered.

He quickly followed up with another, "Cool, do you live there?"

Continuing the small talk, I said, "Technically I live in St. Paul. I've been there for a little over a year. What about you? Where's home for you? Where are you headed?"

Happy to tell me more about himself, he shared, "Fort Lauderdale. That's home for me. But you know, just be glad you don't live in Minnesota. I was flying through there last week, and they got an inch of snow — in the month of MAY! Do you believe that? Too cold for me!"

Wait, what? I started recounting the conversation and reviewing what I said. *Did he not hear me? Maybe he thought I said "Indianapolis?" Was I having a hazy moment where maybe I told him that I lived in one of the other four cities in which I had previously resided and perhaps "Minneapolis" wasn't what actually came out of my mouth? Is he that geographically challenged? In any of these cases, what's my end game? Is it my duty to care whether the man in front of me waiting for coffee knows that Min-neapolis is, in fact, located in the state of Minnesota?*

That day I decided that it may not have been my duty, but we had time. Why not allow him another opportunity to prove to me that he, equipped with his knowledge of major US cities and states, had indeed graduated the fourth grade. I simply pitched him the ball and waited for the home run —*I have faith in you, my friend*.

Enunciating as clearly as I could, I said, "What an adjustment my first year was moving to MMMinneapolis! It snowed so much and was so frigidly cold that I almost couldn't take it. The second year, I think I knew what to expect, so I wasn't so overwhelmed by the climate." The man in line had a more important agenda —to one-up me, "Oh, I'm sure living in Minneapolis was an adjustment, but it's still not Minnesota! I mean, SNOW, in MAY! I just can't get over that!"

I smiled and nodded, remaining silent. I thought to myself, *okay, yeah, that's a strike out. So, geography wasn't his strong suit, but maybe he'd be more successful with multiplication facts instead?*

DID YOU KNOW

Bringing alcohol on board is perfectly fine, but unfortunately, consuming it on board the aircraft is not. Many passengers think the airlines put this rule into effect so that they can make a profit from marked up liquor prices, but this rule is actually an FAA regulation.

If I had to take a stab at the reason why the FAA established the rule, and the reason why airlines charge exorbitant prices for alcohol, I would guess that both the FAA and the airlines are working towards the same goal: keeping passengers safe and comfortable.

One effort to keep everyone safe is having flight attendants regulate the quantity of alcohol that can be consumed by each passenger. Therefore, if the FAA says you can't drink your own alcohol, then by default you must purchase your alcohol from the flight attendants. If the alcohol sold by the flight attendants is expensive, then you might be less likely to purchase more than one or two drinks. Because, you would realize that for the cost of two minis on the airplane, you could have purchased a full-sized bottle on

the ground. Drink responsibly on airplanes —
your liver and your bank account will thank
you.

Con Derri-Air

I am fortunate enough to say that over the course of my career I can count on one hand the number of difficult passengers who ended up being nearly impossible to please. I'm not talking about the type of passenger who requests an extra snack or three drinks. I'm talking about the passenger who has ulterior motives from the start. These are the passengers who always find a way to twist the details of a story to become a victim, or passengers who only accept a remedy to a problem if it aligns with their agendas. Rarely have I experienced these passengers, but when I have, the universe found a way to remind me that kindness is key, and karma will prevail.

My crew and I reached our last leg for the night. We had a short, one-hour flight left to work before we reached our layover city. We arrived at the airplane early preparing for the passengers to board when the gate agent appeared at the aircraft with a lengthy update.

"Hi guys! How are we doing tonight? Could I ask you a favor? Would it be okay if I start the boarding process a few minutes early? I have a passenger who told me that she requires a little more time to get situated. And I must mention, this passenger seems to be quite ornery. She approached me rudely with her demands, telling me she needed the extra time for boarding due to an injury. I told her that was completely fine, but she continued on the defense, telling me that I wasn't permitted to ask about her injury because it was none of my business, even though I *didn't* ever ask about her injury and already told her that she could board the plane at the start of the boarding process. The gate agent from the city she departed from placed a note with high priority in her file to provide all of us with some information. I'll spare you the details, but please be aware that she tends to make a mountain out of a molehill. Based on the notes, it seems like she's no stranger to making a scene."

I couldn't help but think, *Great! I can't wait to deal with this peach, especially at the point in the day when my patience is running thin. Is someone going to end up in a viral video tonight, because I really don't want it to be me.* The flight attendants agreed that boarding a few minutes early would be fine. We are always happy to take any extra steps to get the last flight of the night boarded and on its way as quickly as possible.

Airline employees, especially gate agents, have the patience of saints. Truly, they do! What did this woman do to cause such a big scene? My coworkers are the most empathetic, kind, and patient people I've ever met. Seldom would you find a gate agent that can't deescalate a scenario and work with a passenger to find a way to, at the very least, meet in the middle. For a gate agent to take the time to put a note in someone's file to warn future gate agents and flight attendants of a passenger's behavior, the passenger must have done something that was truly noteworthy. This was the first, and only, time I've ever experienced a warning about a passenger's previous behavior that I should keep an eye out for. Sadly, the agent never explained what the notes in the passenger's file said, but luckily for us, we'd have an experience of our own.

I did, however, want to start with a clean slate. Maybe I'd get along with her swimmingly. Sometimes, the slightest word can be misinterpreted and then the whole dynamic of the situation changes. Therefore, maybe I could bring extra kindness to the situation and assist her so that I win her over and she will be pleasant for the flight. That was the route I would take—killing her with kindness!

Boarding began and the lady appeared at the aircraft door. I welcomed her with a big smile and asked her if I could assist her with any of her items. Her purse and duffle bag seemed manageable, so I was happy to offer an extra service of valeting her items if it would help win her over.

She seemed to be appreciative of the assistance. I helped to get her situated in her seat on the aisle. She was sitting in a unique seat, 4C. If you were to walk down the center aisle of the aircraft, you would first pass the first-class cabin. Directly following first class was the start of the main cabin and this was the row that Ms. Ornery was sitting in.

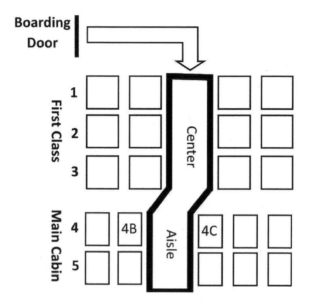

The design of the plane had two seats on one side of the aircraft and three seats on the other side of the aircraft. Because of this lopsided design, once you reach the main cabin, there is a shift of the center aisle such that it jukes to the right and then continues straight back, all the way to the rear. You can see in the diagram that if you would be occupying Seat 4C, a good portion of your legroom would spill into the center aisle. This seat is a great seat while in flight, but probably the most inconvenient seat during the boarding process. The majority of the seats on the aircraft were behind 4C, which meant that people were entering the plane, headed to the back, and were likely to accidentally bump into the passenger sitting there as they made the sharp turn to follow the path of the center aisle.

After getting Ms. Ornery settled into her seat, I wondered how well this location was going to work out for her. She seemed content in her seat, which was a spacious one when void of other passengers. I told her to let me know if there was anything that I could do to assist her. She thanked me for my help, and I thought we just might be able to finish out the day of flying without any extra drama. As I returned to the front of the aircraft, the other passengers began arriving at the end of the jetbridge, ready to board the plane.

We started boarding with the first-class cabin and then welcomed the rest of the passengers on board. During boarding, I assisted with the first-class beverage service offered on the ground prior to departure, so I hadn't yet made my way through the rest of the plane to assist with closing bins or answering passengers' questions. Approximately halfway through the boarding process a call light illuminated. I looked down the aisle and I could see that the light was illuminated in row 4 on the side of the aircraft where Ms. Ornery was sitting. I headed out into the aisle to check on the passengers.

Meeting eyes with Ms. Ornery, I asked her what I could help her with. "I need some ice," she demanded. Naturally, I asked her if everything was okay and she grumbled, "No! There was a passenger that came barreling by with her bag and she smacked directly into my leg. I just had surgery on my left leg and I'm slowly recovering. I can already feel it swelling. I need ice immediately." I, of course, agreed to get her the ice and told her I'd be right back.

I walked up to the galley, retrieved a bag of ice, and headed back to see Ms. Ornery. I provided her with the bag of ice and then began thinking about the rest of the flight and how she would be at risk sitting in 4C for the duration. I wondered if I could find her a seat comparable to the one that she was sitting in that would protect her leg and make it less susceptible to an accidental hit by passersby. A gentleman was sitting in 4B, across the aisle from Ms. Ornery, and since he was well within earshot of our conversations, I decided to include him as a potential part of a solution.

I knelt in front of Ms. Ornery and I explained to her that we would be passing through the cabin with two metal carts when it was time to offer beverages. I explained that we tend to run back and forth to grab supplies and while we always try our best to be respectful of passengers' personal space, there was a possibility that accidental bumps could happen. Additionally, I informed her that passengers would be passing by to use the restroom and this could also create an opportunity for an accident. I thought that having just had a surgery on her left leg, maybe it would be best to have her in an aisle seat that was on the opposite side of the aisle so that her left leg wouldn't have as much exposure to the aisle and would be safer from any other accidental bumps.

I looked over to the gentleman traveling alone and sitting in 4B. I asked if he wouldn't mind swapping aisle seats with Ms. Ornery. Neither passenger would have to move bags or belongings because they were both remaining in the same row; they would simply trade aisle seats. The gentleman in 4B seemed annoyed to have to make the swap, but ultimately agreed to assist my efforts. At that moment, I wasn't sure what seemed to bother him about the situation but would later learn why he seemed resistant.

My efforts were all for nothing because Ms. Ornery declared that she wouldn't be moving seats. She stated that she had chosen this seat specifically to be able to stretch her leg out because she'd be sitting for the duration of the flight. I did my best to convince her to take the seat where her leg would be safer, but she declined my offer again. I assured her that we would do our best to be careful of her leg during the flight.

I knew that there was more to this story, now. A thought ran through my mind. *Why wouldn't she want to do everything she could to protect her more vulnerable leg? This was a one-hour long flight and there was still plenty of legroom to stretch if she took 4B.*

I shared the story with my fellow flight attendants, explaining the events that occurred so that they were caught up to speed. We discussed her surgery, the accidental bump from a passenger while boarding, and the refusal to switch seats. Once in flight, we all took the extra precautions when maneuvering the carts past row 4. We completed the beverage service and we seemed to make it through the entire flight without any more incidents. As the end of the flight was nearing, I heard a chime and noticed the call light illuminated again. I approached Ms. Ornery to see what I could do for her now.

"Yes, I'd like a report," she required, as if I were her personal assistant who should add it to my "To-Do" list.

"I'm sorry, I don't think I understand what you're asking for," I said with a look of confusion on my face.

She cleared up her vague request. "I would like a written incident report to take with me. That woman hit me with her bag, and I need to have a report of what happened. There are certainly going to be medical bills."

I did my best not to let on that I wasn't buying her story and that I thought she was a horrible human being, but I kept my judgments to myself, "Unfortunately, we don't provide incident reports. If you'd like, I can submit a narrative regarding what you've explained to me, which would simply be your account of the situation—whatever you share with me. I, however, can't provide you with any kind of report regarding what happened to you, because I wasn't here to witness the event."

Loving the idea that a captivating narrative could be spun in her voice the way she saw the events occurring, Ms. Ornery agreed, "Yes, you need to submit that narrative and you need to 'CC' me on that e-mail." I don't think she could have been more obvious about her intentions. She's dying to have a paper trail, but she's going to be sadly disappointed.

"Ma'am, my submission isn't in the form of an e-mail and there isn't an option to "CC" you on it, unfortunately. You could write into the Customer Service department to explain the incident and they'll certainly follow up with you," I explained.

"I'm going to need something written formally by you before I get off this plane," she insisted with a slightly threatening tone. Remaining calm and sticking to the truth, I shared that I hated to disappoint her, but I wasn't authorized to put anything in writing. I immediately sensed her dissatisfaction that she wouldn't be getting exactly what she asked for.

The situation seemed to become fishier each time I interacted with her. I provided her a better seat to sit in that would protect her leg and she declined. Now she wanted some sort of formal documentation regarding the incident because she believed there would be medical bills. I was now incredibly suspicious about what exactly happened when this suitcase ran into her.

I was in the galley with one of my colleagues when the gentleman in 4B came to the front of the aircraft to use the lavatory. He pulled my colleague and me aside to give us the scoop, "That woman across the aisle from me never got hit with the suitcase in the way she's making it sound. A young girl was rolling her bag past that lady and one of the wheels ran into her toe because that lady had her feet laid across the aisle. The girl wasn't even moving fast — I would be surprised if she even felt it. The lady across from me didn't even react. She's making this whole thing up. I wasn't trying to be disagreeable when you asked me to switch seats, I just didn't want to play into whatever scheme she's trying to work here."

I didn't want to discuss this type of event with another passenger—it was a slippery slope, regardless if we perceived the situation in the same way. So, we thanked him for giving his account of the story, apologized for inconveniencing him with seat switching, and shared that we were ultimately just glad that no one was hurt. He told us that if we needed him to be a witness to the event, that he would verify the incident never actually happened. He returned to his seat and directly after he sat down, Ms. Ornery, with not even the slightest indication of physical injury, made her way to the front of the aircraft. She used the lavatory, and then found her way back to her seat.

Hearing from the Captain that we should prepare for landing, I stepped into the aisle to collect trash and I saw that the gentleman in 4B was trying to catch my eye. He was giving me that look—the one where he wanted me to take notice of something going on around him without specifically pointing it out. Without drawing attention to the fact that I was looking at Ms. Ornery I peeked across the aisle quickly. Unfortunately, I didn't notice anything out of the ordinary. I gave him a raised eyebrow in return to say, "I'm not seeing what you're seeing." He just started laughing to himself and gestured with his hand to say, "Never mind, don't worry about it." Now, I was even more curious as to what was going on.

After the flight was over, all the passengers began grabbing their belongings and heading off the plane. Knowing that something had happened with Ms. Ornery, I was on the lookout as she deplaned. What was it? Was she writing a nasty letter to give me? Was there something about her leg that he wanted me to notice? I completely missed what he wanted me to see in flight, but now I was on the edge of my seat as I waited for her turn to deplane.

I smiled largely as Ms. Ornery passed by to step off the aircraft. I thanked her for flying with us and wished her a great rest of her evening. She muttered a quick, "Yeah" and turned the corner to exit the aircraft. As she turned the corner, I saw what the gentleman in 4B saw earlier.

When she used the lavatory, she must have also used a toilet seat cover made of thin tissue-type paper. Upon pulling up her pants, half of the seat cover must have got caught inside her underwear, and the other half of the cover was hanging out of her pants like a paper tail. She must have thought that it flushed down the toilet, but she had been dragging it along with her for the rest of the flight.

The gentleman in 4B deplaned very shortly after Ms. Ornery, and he pulled me aside and asked, "Did you see it on the way out? Karma came in the form of a toilet seat cover hanging out of her pants. That's what she gets for trying to be a con artist. Did you notice that not one person around her told her it was there? I know they all saw it, too! Did you see it?" I gave 4B a wink as he stepped off the plane, and I said, "Nope, didn't see a thing! Someone should really tell her about that!"

TRAVEL TIP

Go ahead and kick those shoes off! We know you may choose to remove your footwear to make yourself feel a bit more comfortable, especially on long flights. While you might keep your shoes off to walk into the bathroom at home, we highly recommend that you slip those sneakers back on before entering the airplane lavatory. Chances are that those droplets you see on the lavatory floor aren't residual splashes from overly aggressive handwashing.

Gas Station Goody-Bag

Nowadays, the new standard for most major carriers is to offer only a beverage with a snack choice to expedite service during short flights. Those beverages and snacks can vary from airline to airline, but I think it's safe to say that when flying on a typical flight most passengers wouldn't expect more than a glass of soda and a couple snack options.

But that doesn't stop the passengers from walking on the plane, unprompted, saying, "I'll have the filet mignon and lobster tail." To which, I so desperately wish I could respond, "What you'll have is half a can of Coke, some pretzels, and a seat. Now knock off the dad jokes!" But instead, I just smile and simply say, "Welcome aboard!" Can we all make a pact that we'll never use this line with flight attendants ever again? Please don't put us in the position where we're forced to pretend this is the first time we've heard it. The struggle is real to put on a fake smile and act like it actually made us laugh. Realistically, we'll always be kind, but can you blame us for rolling our eyes once you've turned the corner?

While we have the passengers who order the surf and turf in jest, we also have passengers who walk on board and expect to order food and beverage options that simply aren't available. We try to be understanding of the situation, because when it comes to soft drinks and snacks, pretty much any place you go on the ground—a convenience store, a gas station, or even an airport newsstand—will have a large variety of options. Unfortunately, on a commercial aircraft, we have a limited amount of space to store food and drink items, resulting in a limited amount of choices offered during service.

One evening, I was flying a short flight—only an hour and a half—where my colleagues and I would pass through the cabin with our carts and offer light refreshments to all our passengers. As service began, I realized that I would be sharing a full-sized cart with another male flight attendant. He was soft-spoken, yet approachable. He was welcoming, but slightly reserved—a man of few words. Most importantly, he certainly wasn't rude to passengers by any means. His interactions were warm as he listened to their requests and did his absolute best to satisfy each one. He was the type of guy who didn't need to fill the silence with meaningless chatter and when he decided that he could add something to a conversation, whether profound or humorous, it was something that you wanted to be sure to tune into.

Mr. Reserved and I progressed through a large portion of the cabin and were feeding off each other's positive energy well. Both of us were very calm and kind with each professional interaction. We greeted our passengers as we rolled the cart past each row, smiling and asking them what drinks we could pour for them this evening. We would get the occasional, "What do you have?" and felt compelled to rattle off the variety of sodas, juices and hot drinks that we offered, followed by the snack choices of cookies, peanuts and pretzels.

As we finished serving almost the entire cabin, we slid back to our final rows. Of course, we each focused on the passengers in our respective rows, but being the multi-taskers that we were, we had learned to also be cognizant of what was happening with our colleagues while on the opposite side of the cart. I took the drink orders for my last group of three passengers and I headed back to the cart to begin pouring the sodas that they ordered.

While standing there waiting for the fizz to calm, I became privy to an interaction between Mr. Reserved and the lady on the aisle he was serving. He approached the lady on the aisle with a "Hello" and then asked how she was doing. She responded, "Hey, I'm good," and before he could offer to serve her a beverage or a snack, she continued with her order. "Let me get a root beer and a cinnamon roll." Leaning back a slight bit, he asked, "Would you like a pack of Marlboro lights and $10 on Pump 11, as well?" He didn't miss a beat and after watching all his kind interactions, I was shocked to find out that he was even able to muster up all that sass.

I had completely burst into laughter. The comment caught me off guard. I certainly wasn't expecting those words to come out of his mouth, so I was obviously tickled and needed to take a moment to compose myself. The lady on the aisle seemed to be confused, not understanding the joke, not understanding why Mr. Reserved hadn't begun putting together her gas station goody-bag, and voicing an audible, "Huh?"

Mr. Reserved tried to clear up the confusion. "It was just a little joke. Never mind, it didn't land," he explained. I think he's wrong. Where I was standing it absolutely landed because I was still laughing. He continued, "I'm sorry, miss, we unfortunately don't have root beer. Can I get you a Coke instead?" She was fine with the substitution, so Mr. Reserved moved on, "And may I get you a snack — cookies, pretzels or peanuts?"

"Are you out of cinnamon rolls? I thought I heard that you were offering cinnamon rolls," she questioned. I thought to myself, *What airline has ever offered cinnamon rolls as a complimentary snack for the main cabin? Have I been missing out this whole time?* Mr. Reserved, refraining from confusing the lady with any more of his jokes, chose a more direct answer. "A cinnamon roll does sound good to me right now, too, but no, I think you may have heard us offer the cookies—they're cinnamon flavored."

The lady was happy with the cookies, so Mr. Reserved passed her both the cookies and the Coke she previously ordered, unlocked the cart brake, and signaled to me with a smile and an eye-roll that it was time to close up shop for the day. As we rolled away past the last row of passengers, he mouthed to me, "Cinnamon rolls?! What that fuck?" and I just shook my head while continuing to laugh.

Did You Know

Most airlines have a nifty little magazine in each seat pocket that includes a page listing all the beverages they offer during their service. Also, some airlines place individual menu cards directly in the pocket so that you can easily locate all the drink options available. If you have a craving for something and you're not sure if the flight attendants have that item on their carts, feel free to check one of the menu options or specifically request the beverage anyway. Because, when you ask, "What do you have?" you'll likely hear, "I have a cart full of sodas, juices, and hot drinks, as well as 100 other people to serve. What do you like?"

Coffee Accountability

Monday morning, bright and early, I waited in the gate area as the time to board the flight was approaching. The 7:00 A.M. flight looked like it would be a full one today, so as a standby traveler commuting to work, I resorted to the jumpseat to be sure I would make my sign-in time for my trip. This simply meant that I would occupy one of the extra flight attendant seats for the duration of the flight, due to no available passenger seats. Ready to head to work, I stepped up to the gate agent to check-in and I requested the jumpseat for the flight.

As I waited for the gate agent to finish up the proper paperwork, one of the flight attendants who would be working the flight reentered the gate area. She spoke to the other gate agent telling him that there had been a problem with the hot water system on the aircraft. Because of this, the flight attendants wouldn't be able to serve any coffee or tea.

The flight attendant thought it would be courteous to inform the passengers in the gate area of their inability to provide hot drinks in flight. Because it was quite early on a Monday morning, many of the passengers would be expecting a cup of coffee to kickstart the day. By sharing this information with everyone in the gate area, passengers could make the decision to find a coffee or tea at one of the airport cafés prior to boarding the plane.

After learning about the situation regarding the hot drinks, which was approximately 55 minutes prior to departure, the gate agent decided to make an announcement as the flight attendant suggested. "Folks, the flight attendants have just made us aware that due to an inoperative hot water system, they will not be able to serve any hot drinks on today's flight. If you had planned to order a coffee or tea on board, we still have a few more moments before we begin boarding. A great option might be to step over to the café directly across from our gate if you're looking for some caffeine this morning. We do apologize for this inconvenience."

More passengers arrived and the gate area became full. Attempting to reach as many passengers as possible, the gate agent repeated his hot drinks announcement nearly verbatim two more times. Following the announcements, I noticed that five or six passengers took advantage of the gate's proximity to the coffee shop by leaving the gate area, stepping in line, and placing their orders. Some of the more seasoned travelers quickly grabbed their drinks from the café counter and ran to the gate to scan their boarding passes right before the door was about to close, efficiently making good use of the remaining five minutes.

Boarding wrapped up and I headed onto the plane to get comfortable in my seat in the back galley. During the last few minutes of boarding, I chatted with one of the flight attendants and our conversation was interrupted by an announcement that welcomed passengers on board. The lead flight attendant stood at the boarding door smiling and offering up some general announcements. Upon completing her warm welcome, she added an extra announcement. "And in addition to welcoming you all aboard, we do want to apologize for our inability to serve hot drinks on today's flight. Hopefully, everyone heard the announcements that the gate agent made while out in the gate area and you were all able to get coffee or tea from the nearby café. Our water system is not working properly and while we have plenty of bottled water on the aircraft, we don't have a way to heat it for coffee or tea. We apologize for this inconvenience and thank you for your understanding."

After boarding was complete and just a short bit after the first announcement, the Captain also took to the PA system to offer his own welcome. "Good morning, folks! Thanks for joining us! We should have a smooth flight today, but we want to offer our apologies regarding the hot water system. The problem is much more involved than our maintenance crew here is equipped to handle. This aircraft will be serviced fully when we land, but we didn't want to delay your flight to try to fix the hot water system now. We know it's important for you to get to your destination on time so that everyone makes their connections. We do apologize, again, for the inconvenience and welcome you aboard!"

We reached the end of the boarding process and by that point the passengers had had five different opportunities to receive the information that this flight would not have any hot water or hot drinks available due to a problem with the water system. I heard three of the announcements made in the gate area, and since I had been on board the aircraft, two additional announcements had been made. While I understood that the information became less useful to our passengers once on the aircraft, the information was still relayed to all of them and apologies were extended several times. Every passenger should have heard this announcement at least once over the course of the last hour.

In flight, I was sitting on the jumpseat in the galley sipping a soda. I wasn't in uniform yet, as I had a few hours before I started my working trip, so I planned to change into work clothes once we landed. Not in uniform, I may have appeared to be a passenger just like all the rest, except that I wore my crew identification badge hanging around my neck for all to see. I occupied a double jumpseat, meaning two flight attendants could safely sit there together, and the other half of the seat was unoccupied. Not having realized that I was a flight attendant, a woman sat down beside me on the jumpseat and said, "Hey, I guess you're here waiting for coffee too? Ugh, I'm dying for a cup. I can't keep my eyes open."

I thought, *Is she serious? She can't really think that I'm back here waiting for coffee. They made at least five announcements about not having hot drinks.* My crew badge was laid over my chest but was secured inside the harness that buckled me in. I reached under the harness to pull my badge out as a hint to her that I was a flight attendant and there was a reason I was sitting in this jumpseat. I certainly wasn't waiting for coffee that wasn't ever going to appear on this flight.

This Coffee Queen didn't seem to notice that my badge revealed my identity and my reason for being in this seat, but I'm not surprised because based on her comment, she hadn't noticed much of anything going on around her this morning. I could understand if the gate agent only made one announcement and she had missed it, but at least five announcements were made—FIVE! She had to have heard at least one of them, whether on or off the airplane.

At the same time the Coffee Queen stunned me with her obliviousness, a gentleman was standing outside the lavatory waiting his turn to enter. The lavatory was adjacent to the galley, so anyone waiting to enter the lavatory would also have been privy to conversations or happenings in the galley. By default, he became part of the conversation offering backup when I would unfortunately have to be the bearer of bad news. "Miss, I'm sitting back here because I'm a flight attendant and there weren't any passenger seats available. So, this is my assigned seat when I'm commuting to work. Also, there won't be any hot drinks on this flight because the hot water system isn't working properly. May I get you a soda if you're looking for a caffeine boost?"

You would have thought that I had told her that I killed her cat. Coffee Queen in disbelief responded, "Are you kidding me? You're for real right now? They don't have any coffee on this plane? It's so freaking early in the morning. How do they not have coffee on the plane? It would have been nice to have a warning beforehand. I can't believe this."

The gentleman stepped in, "Miss, didn't you hear any of the announcements?"

"They didn't make any announcements!" she said defensively.

"Well, that's false. I heard the gate agent make two out in the gate area and then the flight attendant made one when we got on. I think even the pilot said something about it, too. There were, like, four announcements or something," the gentleman provided as evidence.

She smugly responded, "Well, I didn't hear them. They should have texted us."

Rolling his eyes, the gentleman criticized, "A text message regarding coffee? That seems like a bit much. I think plenty of people took advantage of the coffee shop across from our gate after the announcements."

Hoping to calm the escalation between the two, I stepped in to address the Coffee Queen, "I'm sorry you weren't made aware of the lack of coffee. Can I grab you a soda or juice?"

"Well, can I have a hot tea, then?" she asked.

I looked at the waiting gentleman while biting my upper lip and he returned the look with a raised eyebrow. Our nonverbal reactions asked one another who was going to be the one that had to explain to her that hot tea is, in fact, a hot drink that also wouldn't be offered today. Before I could form a polite response, the waiting gentleman barreled through. He laughed to soften his abrasiveness, "What about the words 'no hot drinks' is confusing? I think that means no hot tea either," he simplified.

The Coffee Queen, disgusted, conceded by saying, "Whatever, then I guess I'll do an iced coffee." At that moment, the lavatory freed up, and the waiting gentleman gracefully bowed out with an exaggerated "Wowww!" signaling that he was throwing in the towel. He couldn't get through to this woman. Sadly, I agreed with his sentiments, but felt I should try to, at least, explain. She just wasn't understanding that no versions of coffee or tea would be available.

Giving a valiant effort, I watered down my explanation. "To make an iced coffee or an iced tea, we would brew hot coffee or hot tea as normal and then simply pour the hot beverages over ice. So, with the hot water system not working, the flight attendants, unfortunately, will not be able to make an iced coffee or iced tea, either. I'm sorry, miss," I explained.

I think my explanation made some sense to her because she blurted out, "Well, that sucks!"

I tried to redirect the conversation towards what I could offer instead of what I couldn't. I apologized and asked her if she wanted a soda or juice, as I had offered before. "Well, do you have orange juice, and is it fresh-squeezed orange juice?" she inquired. I decided it was time to defer the question to the working flight attendants.

Of course, I knew that the juice wasn't fresh squeezed, but I had exhausted my patience and I hadn't even started my workday yet. I needed to reserve my patience for when I would be on the clock. I encouraged her to return to her seat where I knew the flight attendants would be able to serve her so that she wouldn't miss her opportunity to get a beverage.

The waiting gentleman exited the lavatory and stepped into the galley asking, "Do you have to deal with people like her all the time?"

I tried to contain my laughter as he curiously asked, "What did she end up deciding to drink?" I indulged him, "Her most recent request was for a glass of orange juice — fresh-squeezed, but I realized it would be best for her to be served by the flight attendants that are working the beverage carts in the aisle right now. I didn't want to step on their toes."

He laughed and while walking away he said, "I'm shocked. So, she went straight for the fresh-squeezed juice. I thought for sure hot chocolate would have been the next request out of her mouth." I have no idea what the Coffee Queen ended up ordering from the flight attendants, but I can guarantee that whatever drink she chose was served cold and was not fresh squeezed.

FREQUENTLY ASKED QUESTIONS

Will you help me with my bag?

Will I help you with your bag? Absolutely! Will I lift it for you by myself? Nope! I always tell passengers that if they start by lifting, I'm happy to help offer a boost so that we can all safely work together to get the bag stowed. If I lift your bag for you, then that means I would have to be willing to lift every passenger's bag. For one flight alone, that could be upwards of 200 bags. Think about how some people pack. I've genuinely questioned if some passengers were transporting gold bars in their suitcases. Would you want to lift 200 of those bags? My health insurance benefits are good, but not *that* good.

Crab Cakes and Wedding Rings

Having a high-maintenance passenger on a flight is, unfortunately, more common than you would think. But if you can work some magic and find a way to win over that passenger, you're likely to make the three hours you have to spend together much more tolerable — dare I say, even enjoyable? A bonus is that the airline you work for will love you forever now that you've made a lifelong customer out of this difficult passenger.

Being the ambitious, fresh, new flight attendant that I was, I had every intention of building a relationship with the passenger in seat 4C who I knew was going to be quite a challenge. From the moment that this woman stepped foot on the aircraft, I could tell that she was going to require much more attention than most passengers typically do.

"Good afternoon, ma'am! Welcome aboard! How are you today?" is exactly what I said when I greeted Granny with a warm, full smile as she boarded the plane. Granny returned my genuine greeting with a diminishing grunt that, loosely translated to the English language, probably would have been, "Don't talk to me and leave me alone."

If you've ever made the effort to address someone and offer a warm welcome, it's natural to feel angry or belittled when a passenger ignores you or worse, offers a grunt. Usually when I get that kind of response from a passenger, I pretend they've said something like, "I'm well, thank you, how are you?" Over time, I've taught myself to create these substitute responses in my head because I very much like my job and I find that keeping the thoughts to myself rather than allowing my sharp tongue to take over, will ensure I remain employed.

Directly following Grunting Granny was her husband, who had been tasked with carrying all their belongings on board. He caught the interaction I'd just had with Granny, and I assume he recognized the immediate deflation in my demeanor. He greeted me with a simple eyebrow raise, which I interpreted as, "I'm sorry she was rude to you. I've been living with it for 40 years. If it makes you feel any better, it's how she treats me all the time, too." They headed to their seats in 4C and 4D, part of our first-class cabin, and made themselves comfortable after Grandpa had stowed all the couple's items to Grunting Granny's liking.

Grunting Granny and Grandpa were that couple who had made their money early on and swiftly retired to their home in Florida. They would tell you that age is just a number and would never pass up a challenge to a tennis match, for which GG appeared to be dressed. She was wearing a crisp white polo with a pale pink signature logo accompanying her skort. To complete her look GG wore a sun visor on the plane with pride — a fashion accessory holdover from her Tuesday golf outings with the gals. I believe she mostly wore it to corral her unmanageable curly white locks that she had permed every couple of months at the upscale salon within the walls of their gated community. Grandpa's outfit, less polished, was a pair of khaki golf shorts and a bright blue polo with a sloppily stretched collar that I can only assume was a direct result of GG yanking around her old ball-and-chain during their day of travel.

Seeing Grandpa barely managing to lug their carry-ons onto the plane confirmed my suspicions around the reason for the weathered condition of his shirt collar. Having been shot down by Grunting Granny and having shared a pitiful moment of eye contact with Grandpa, I had a pretty good idea who I was dealing with and what to expect on this flight. I decided to redirect my positive energy towards the other passengers coming on board. Once we were airborne, the real fun could begin as I would have the honor to provide excellent service to people who are rude to you for absolutely no reason.

As soon as our aircraft reached an altitude of 10,000 feet and it was safe for the flight attendants to begin cabin service, we each began checking items off our "to-do" lists. All the flight attendants had specific responsibilities on this flight, and one of mine was to prepare most of the food and drink items in the front galley. On today's menu were two meal choices for first class: crab cakes — the hot option, and a grilled chicken salad — the cold one. I turned on the oven, programmed the temperature to the medium setting, and punched in a timer for 16 minutes to be sure the crab cakes would be warmed throughout. I moved on to unwrapping the cling wrap that sealed in the fixings on each tray and was sure that all the glassware was ready for a beautiful lunch at 32,000 feet in the air.

While I was busy in the galley, the Lead Flight Attendant put in more face time with the passengers by taking drink and food orders, thanking them for their business, and conversing about the day and their travel experiences. The Lead Flight Attendant's lengthy amount of time spent in the aisle with passengers became noticeable when I realized that I had completed my tasks and was ready to begin plating meals before she had even returned to the galley.

I peeked my head around the corner to look down the aisle and I could see that the Lead Flight Attendant was planted at seats 4C and 4D, where she appeared to be offering apologies. Something had upset Grunting Granny, and my colleague had become the punching bag for her frustrations. The Lead Flight Attendant wrapped up the interaction and headed in my direction. She seemed a little rattled, but she managed to keep her composure as she pulled me to the side. She informed me that she'd had an upsetting encounter with Granny, and she encouraged me to be cognizant of my interactions with her.

Working as a team, any time we can give each other warning of a potentially explosive situation, we do! In this case, my Lead Flight Attendant wanted me to be sure I was extra attentive to Granny's needs and to offer her the best service I could. Naturally, after my negative interaction with Granny during the boarding process, I had much curiosity regarding the conversation she had just shared with the Lead Flight Attendant.

My colleague recounted their exchange with me. She told me that when she asked the couple if they would care for lunch, Grunting Granny, or GG for short, demanded to know what the options for lunch would be. Kneeling next to GG's seat, she explained, "Well, we do have a limited amount of each option on board, and unfortunately, we have run out of one of the options. We have a lovely grilled chicken salad still available. Would you care to have the salad today?"

GG snapped back, "No. No, I absolutely wouldn't care for a chicken salad. What's the other option?" The Lead Flight Attendant hesitantly shared the requested information knowing the second option wasn't an option at all. "Well, my other option was crab cakes, but as I mentioned previously, I have a limited number of each and having taken the orders of the passengers sitting in front of you, I unfortunately do not have both options left. I apologize, but I don't have any more crab cakes to offer. I wish I had more so that all passengers could have their first choice," she explained regretfully. My immediate reaction was, *What was the point in knowing the other option if it wasn't available, anyway? Was GG a glutton for punishment?*

"Well, I paid for a seat in first class. I expect a hot meal," GG exclaimed. The Lead Flight Attendant assured GG that she would absolutely provide her with a meal, but it would have to be a salad, as that was the only option left. Unfortunately, GG wouldn't accept that response and boldly stated that she didn't want the salad! "I'm sorry, ma'am, it's the only option I have left," said the Lead Flight Attendant. She reached a dead end with possible options.

GG didn't back down, "Well, I'm going to eat on this flight," she declared with arrogance. "Okay. So, you're going to eat the salad," the Lead Flight Attendant confirmed. "I apologize again. Grandpa, would you care for lunch? A salad for you as well?" Grandpa was happy accepting the salad.

Thanks to the Lead Flight Attendant's heads up, I knew that I might need to walk on eggshells a bit when I visited the couple in the aisle to take their drink orders. I took a deep breath, smacked a smile on my face, and headed straight to row 4 to offer drinks to our favorite passengers. "Just give me water, you probably ran out of anything that I'd like anyway," GG barked. I ignored her snide remark and agreed to bring her water, then asked, "What's your drink of choice, though? I'd love to bring it out to you if I have it onboard!"

"What I really want is a margarita, but I know you can't make that," she huffed. Excited that I could fulfill her request, I shared with GG that I had all the ingredients and that I would be more than happy to make it for her! I convinced her that she would really enjoy it! Pleasantly surprised that I had something that she wanted she agreed, "Well, that actually sounds lovely. Yes, I'd love one."

Attempting to reach some common ground with GG, I decided to see if I couldn't keep the positive conversation flowing about margaritas. "I don't know if you're anything like me, but I love sugar on the rim of my margarita. And if you're not a fan of sugar, I could use the same strategy to rim the glass with salt! Now, it's not the fancy sanding sugar or salt you'd get at a Mexican restaurant, but I do have sugar and salt packets and I can make it happen either way you like," I offered.

Changing her tune, "I *knew* I liked you! I'm a sugar gal, too! Sugar on the rim would be lovely. Something about the tartness of the lime and the sweetness of the sugar! It's perfect!" I acknowledged GG's accurate description of the combination and then reveled in knowing that I had her on my side, even if it was just for a moment. I took Grandpa's drink order and then I worked my way back to the galley with the orders in hand.

I headed into the galley with a smile on my face. Finally, I had found some way to make this woman happy! I shared with the Lead Flight Attendant that I had won GG over simply by bonding over our preferences for alcohol consumption. Then the realization hit: I was going to have to attempt to sugar the rim on the glass of GG's margarita. I had absolutely no idea how I was going to logistically accomplish this using the materials and workspace in one of the smallest galleys in the entire airline's fleet. The galley is not equipped with rimming rings in which we can dip margarita glasses—but where there's a will, there's got to be a way!

I found myself gently rotating GG's glass while I poured a spoonful of margarita mix over the glass' rim. Then I sprinkled the sugar packets on the sticky mix, hoping that some of the granules would adhere to the glass and make the fine crystal resemble a classic margarita. I scooped in some ice, added the tequila, and then topped the glass off with margarita mix, a splash of soda, and orange juice for a little something extra. I finished it off with a garnish of lime—presentation is everything, right?

I quickly poured a glass of Coke for Grandpa, and I placed both beverages on the tray to head back out to serve our passengers. I approached the couple and announced, "All right! Here we go! I have a Coke for you, sir, and a margarita with a sugared rim for you, miss." GG skeptically looked at the glass as she thanked me and shared that she was interested to see how it would taste.

I anxiously awaited as she took the first sip, unsure if I were about to receive a verbal lashing for not enough sugar or too much mix. As I stood there waiting, I had the realization that my makeshift margarita might not align with GG's expectations. Easing my concerns, GG exclaimed, "This is delicious! I love that mix! What's the brand? I'd love to buy it when I get back home!"

Finally exhaling at her positive reaction, I said, "I'll write down the brand for you, so you have it to take with you! I'm so glad you're enjoying it. We have plenty on-board! Please let me know if you need anything else."

After I dropped off a napkin with the brand name scribbled on it for GG, the Lead Flight Attendant and I contin-

ued serving meals and beverages to the first-class cabin. As
we periodically checked in on all the passengers, I noticed
that GG's glass was more than half-empty, and I instantly
took the approach that hell hath no fury like a high-maintenance woman sober. I immediately ran to the galley to
make a second margarita on the rocks, rimmed with sugar
and garnished with lime. When I delivered her refill, surprisingly, I received a smile from GG—a real, genuine, appreciative, and almost kind smile. I felt like I'd won a
million dollars. This grouchy woman who I thought would
be a thorn in my side for the duration of our three-hour
flight had completely changed her tune with a glass of sug-
ary lime juice and a shot of tequila. She had softened and
she appeared to be enjoying her flight.

A short time later, I checked on GG and I noticed that
she was finishing up her second beverage. On longer flights,
I don't find it uncommon to offer a third or even fourth
drink to a passenger, as long as the drinks aren't being
slammed down. GG seemed to be able to hold her liquor
well and was exhibiting no signs of intoxication—as far as I
knew she'd only had two drinks within the last two hours.
She politely accepted a third margarita, saying, "Yes, I'd love
another one, but there's no rush, honey. I'm going to use the
restroom in just a moment, so whenever you have a chance,
that would be great!" I perceived her term of endearment
as a little victory, and I assured her that her honey would be
happy to pour her another one—I'd have it right out.

GG headed into the lavatory, which is directly adjacent
to the front galley. While she was away from her seat, I

crafted her another one of my signature margaritas and delivered it so that it would be waiting for her at her seat when she returned. Grandpa smiled at me and I could tell he was so grateful to see that we were doing everything that we could to make his wife happy. He obviously had to deal with the nastiness and the frustrations that she had no problem voicing whenever she was unhappy. Feeling proud that I seemed to be handling everything smoothly, I headed back to the galley to tidy up the mess I had just made with the sugar packets while making margarita #3.

After cleaning up my mess and wiping down the galley counters, I took a quick moment to relax. Our passengers were content, and our crew had accomplished all components of cabin service. Alone in the galley, I watched as GG exited the lavatory and took a step toward me. "You're fantasssstic! No, really! Reallllly! You are wonnnnnderful!" she slurred. "Aww, well, that's very nice of you to say. I just wanted to make sure you had a nice experience with us, and I know you didn't get your first choice of meals. I wanted to make sure you were taken care of." I explained.

Feeling less inhibited, GG began expressing her remorse. "I have to say. I just have to say it. I apologize. And please, PLEASE, apologize to the Lead Flight Attendant for me. I need to say sorry to her. I'll say sorry to her when she comes back. I need to say sorry to her because she is sooo nice. But will you apologize to her for me?" she asked. I agreed that the Lead Flight Attendant was nice and a pleasure to work with, and I would be happy to pass along a message for her.

Each word slurred out more sloppily than the last as GG instructed, "Pleeease tell her that I'm sorry for giving her a hard time. She was jussst trying to offer me what she had for food options and it's not herrrr fault that she didn't have enough." I told GG that I really appreciated her apology and understanding of the situation, and that I would be happy to pass the apology on to my colleague. I also assured her that I understood wanting one option and only being offered the other. I recognized that could be disappointing.

GG wouldn't hear it. She was ready to take full responsibility, "No, no, NO! It was myyy fault! I overreacted! Honey let me tell you! It all started this morning when I woke up, looked in the mirror, and this giant zit appeared on my face. It was all downhill from there."

Trying to ease her insecurities, I said, "Oh, I didn't even notice it." I was lying. I totally noticed it.

"Well *I* noticed it and it ruined my morning. We love flying on you guys, but our second flight tonight is delayed getting to the West Coast, and if we would have known earlier today, then we could have adjusted our morning flight. I know flight delays happen. It's okay . . . ya know, it's reallly okay. It's just that I found out when I got to the airport that our layover between flights would be five hours. That's five hours I could have spent on the beach. So, when I got on the plane, I just wasn't happy at all. Then, that poor woman came over to offer me lunch and I gave her a terribly hard time," GG admitted.

She then took a step closer to me. By this point, she was uncomfortably close. She had officially hit the point in her alcohol consumption where she didn't honor personal space. She took no note that she was a mere 6 to 7 inches away from my face and continued, "I told that woman. I told that pooor woman that I was going to eat on this flight! And I asked her what other option she had even though I knew well and good that she didn't have any more of that option to offer me. And you know what?!" I obliged and asked, "What?" In an attempt to whisper which just translated to a breathy scream, she yelled, "Crab Cakes! Her other option was CRAB CAKES! I gave her a hard time and YOU. KNOW. WHAT?! I don't even liiike crab cakes!"

I made a valiant effort to hold back explosive laughter, but a giggle slipped out, which I quickly used as a transition to lighten the mood: "Oh, don't worry. I'm sure she understands, and I find it hard to believe you gave her a hard time!" But I thought, *Let's face facts, I absolutely can believe you gave the Lead Flight Attendant a hard time.* GG assured me that she did. She continued stressing how terribly she had acted and how she hoped that she could be forgiven for treating my colleague so poorly.

Then, GG had grabbed onto my arm — I'm not sure if the tequila had released a touchy-feely monster or if she just needed a pillar of stability upon which to sturdy herself. Either way, I found this interaction utterly humorous, and while I normally don't care for passengers touching me, GG's remorse had altered the way I viewed her. The wicked witch I'd perceived earlier had transformed into this sweet older woman who had seen the error in her ways, apologized, and chose to make further amends. I assured her that everything was great, I would pass on her sincerest apologies, and there would be no hard feelings. Once I managed to separate from GG, the flight remained uneventful until a call light signaled.

I looked down the aisle and saw that my new best friend sitting in 4C had rung her call light and was frantically trying to get my attention. "Frantic" barely begins to describe the sense of urgency in GG's wild gesticulations; for a moment, I had concerns that her seat had become a pit of quicksand and if she didn't have my immediate assistance, she would easily be sucked into suffocation. I bolted over to her seat, fully expecting her to explain that she was flailing her arms and waving me down because her husband was having a heart attack or wasn't breathing.

It was quite the contrary: I found Grandpa sleeping as peacefully as a baby, and directed my undivided attention to GG as she appeared to have instantaneously sobered and was now begging me to come closer for what I was sure to be her deepest, darkest secret. She whispered to me in yet another breathy scream, "OH! MY! GOD! I lost my wedding ring! I need your help! PLEASE! I can't wake him up! If he finds out I lost that ring, he'll murder me! You think I'm kidding?! His lawyers will meet the flight to serve me divorce papers as I walk off this plane. PLEASE, will you help me look?!"

"Of course I will!" I responded.

My initial reaction was to laugh. Was this real? I had always been told that some days flying would be more exciting than others. Today, I felt like I had been transported to a Thursday night sitcom that we all assumed would have a happy ending, but only after the dynamic duo of Flight Attendant and Grunting Granny found themselves in the strangest, funniest, and grossest scenarios. Prime time TV had begun. "Why don't we start with your seat cushion?" I suggested to my sitcom sidekick. "The cushion itself is attached with some Velcro. It should be easy to pull up. I bet you didn't think you were going to practice using your flotation device today, did you?!"

"No kidding!" GG replied. "I also didn't expect to be single at this age, which is what I'm going to be if I don't find that ring!" With a chuckle, I assured her that everything would be okay, and we would find the ring. I hoped we would, at least. GG and I slowly pulled the bottom seat cushion up from the rest of the metal frame of her seat. She made sure I helped her do it slowly, so as not to wake her sleeping hubby with the ripping sound of the Velcro separating. I got the seat cushion pulled up and she could dive into the foundation of the seat and shove her fingers in the small crevices to feel around for her lost ring.

"Ms. GG," I said, "it looks like you have some room now to poke around here. Why don't I leave you here to look around your seat while I start looking in the lavatory to see if I can find it in there? Maybe it slipped off when you were washing your hands." She agreed, "That's a great idea! Thank you so much, I'll keep looking,"

I left GG and row 4 with a hopeful smile, only to realize that this ring could be in other areas of the lavatory aside from the sink where she had washed her hands. I went back to the galley to prepare myself mentally and physically. I found and put on a pair of nylon gloves, rolled my sleeves up, and took a big breath, reminding myself that I was being a good person by helping this lady.

As anyone who's traveled in an airplane knows, the lavatory on board is incredibly small—the tight quarters wouldn't really allow for much movement while I was searching for a small ring in there, so I decided to leave the door wide open while I investigated. My strategy was to approach the "safe" areas first, in hopes that the ring would still be within view and I wouldn't have to dig my heels into the nitty gritty of the airplane restroom. I'd already established in my head that the toilet was off limits—if that's where it had fallen, she'd be out of luck because I was certainly not sticking my hand in there.

So, I started with the small, metal box-like frame that held a short stack of paper towels and was attached to the countertop. I reached inside to feel around for anything that might be GG's precious jewelry. Nope! Nothing. I looked at the sink stopper, jiggling it a bit and assessing whether the opening where the water would drain would be wide enough for a ring to slide down. I decided that the ring more than likely wouldn't have been able to fit through the gap, but I'd pull the stopper up just to cover my bases. The stopper slid out with ease, but all I could see was the dark and narrow drain. This attempt appeared to have been unsuccessful. Having no desire to pursue this any further, I decided to try a different route.

Maybe GG had removed her ring to wash her hands, set it on the counter, and, after drying her hands, accidentally pushed the ring into the garbage chute with the paper towel she disposed of. I felt around for the latch to open the trash compartment under the sink and pulled out the tall rectangular container that catches garbage from the chute. With the trash can out of the way, I looked around the pipes and other components, only to discover that the ring hadn't been hiding there. Naturally, the next step would be to go through the trash can and be sure the ring wasn't mixed in with the soggy paper towels and other fun treats that passengers discard while in the restroom.

I grabbed a larger waste bag and opened it, transferring all of the soggy paper towels and other passenger trash into the larger waste bag to be absolutely certain that I had combed through every possible item that could be concealing this ring. I meticulously picked up every individual paper towel and ran my fingers along it, squeezing as I went, to be sure her ring wasn't stuck inside. I wasn't having any luck, but I continued looking because I'd promised GG that everything was going to be all right!

Everything *was* all right, except for maybe my dignity. I found myself kneeling with half of my body on the lavatory floor, peering out into the aisle through the crack at the hinge. Fortunately for me, in that moment, that gap provided me with a direct sightline to GG. I looked up and saw nothing other than her legs and backside sticking out into the aisle because she, like me, was on all fours, looking everywhere she could to find this ring. I shoved my hand into the garbage can for one last swoop, elbow deep. As I did, I saw GG, whom I had never imagined to be as spry as she was, jump up to her feet and, with a full voice, scream two words: "FOUND IT!"

Everyone on the plane was now suffering from whiplash because of how quickly they snapped their necks left, right, and up to identify the reason for the startling scream, and rightfully so. GG screamed as excitedly as if she had just found one of Willy Wonka's golden tickets, and because of it, Grandpa was no exception to the group suffering from whiplash. As you'd probably expect, GG's exclamation had awakened him from his nap. My curiosity had taken over, and instead of cleaning up the disaster of trash that I'd been picking through, I carelessly pushed it all into the lavatory and out of the way so that I could bolt over to GG and find out where the ring had been hiding.

GG saw me and repeated, "I found it!"

"I'm so happy you were able to find it. Was it on the floor?" I was dying to know.

GG explained, "No. Right before I left the restroom, I pumped some lotion onto my hands, but I wanted to take my ring off before I rubbed it in. So, when I came back to my seat, I placed the ring in that little section of the seat pocket while I moisturized. I completely forgot that I never put my ring back on and that I had stored it there for safe keeping. It wasn't until later that I realized it was missing, and by that time, I had forgotten that I had taken it off. Oh, my goodness." She let out an excessive sigh. "After all of that, I'm going to need another drink." Standing in front of her with my still-gloved, trash-covered hands, I said, "You're going to need two more drinks, because you're having one for me, as well."

TRAVEL TIP

What's more important than comfort on a long flight? Before heading to the airport think about items that would help you relax or that might help you fall asleep more easily. Items like ear plugs, pillows, blankets, Xanax, and eye masks are great accessories to carry with you. Don't worry though, if you happen to forget your eye mask, the lavatories offer free feminine care panty-lining pads that will do the trick. You wouldn't be the first person I've seen do it, just sayin'!

It Takes a Village

I think that the single-most frustrating component of flying for passengers is relinquishing control over travel — air travel is unlike any other form of transportation. The frustration resulting from the lack of control can manifest itself in the form of snarky comments, misdirected anger, or just sheer nervousness. Having flown plenty of times while working and as a passenger, I recognize that none of these manifestations are personal attacks against me. Nor are these kinds of behavior a fair representation of a passenger's character.

To regain some control of the situation, passengers spend quite a bit of time focusing on reaching their ultimate level of comfort in an environment that is anything but comfortable for most. Working towards that goal gives passengers a chance to take control over some portion of their travel experience. So, they might choose to sneak both carry-on items into the overhead bin to clear extra legroom, or board as early as possible to commandeer elbow space on the armrest. On most every flight, passengers are focused on themselves and what they can do to make their own experience more comfortable and enjoyable.

This flight was different. This flight opened my eyes to the way that a group of strangers could come together for a common goal, and not necessarily in the way I had expected. I had just worked my last flight of the day and the final leg of the rotation was a deadheading leg back to my base, so I was just flying home sitting in a passenger seat. I ran to the bathroom to change into civilian clothes, then I nestled myself into my window seat. Headphones were in and I was ready to lean against the window for a nap knowing that I was heading home for a few days off.

Passengers were filing onto the plane and the gate agent was nearly ready to close the door. The two seats next to me weren't filled yet. I wondered if I might have a little extra room to spread out on this flight. With just a couple minutes left before the boarding door was shut, a family boarded and two of the members sat next to me. The first passenger was a young mother, in her early thirties and noticeably exhausted. There was no way she could hide the deep, dark rings under her eyes. Her exhaustion wasn't a slight look of fatigue from a restless night's sleep. She looked as if she lived each day functioning under some level of exhaustion. Joining her was an active boy, maybe 7 or 8 years old, full of curiosity and energy.

Mom sat in the aisle seat, and the boy began settling into the middle seat, buckling in next to me. Mom stowed all of her and her son's belongings while she also provided a barrier to keep him from exiting our row. In what seemed like a flash of energy, maybe four seconds in total, the boy unbuckled, stood up, yanked on the seat in front of him, sat down, reached across my body to raise and lower the window shade, and then fumbled with his seat belt again. In an instant, I understood the look of exhaustion on the mother's face.

For the first few moments that the two were getting acclimated with the seat and the functions of the entertainment system built into it, the boy seemed to be occupied. Games and shows on the in-seat monitor seemed to intrigue him and the ability to touch the screen just like a tablet or smartphone made the monitor accessible and familiar. That was, until Lead Flight Attendant made an announcement that created a system-wide pause in functionality on the screen, which was an unavoidable safety measure to be sure all passengers knew to focus on the announcement. The boy became irate, and not in a way where he was yelling expletives or crying tears. He showed his emotions through his physical movements. He began punching the monitor and kicking the seat in front of him with the same incredible force and pace as a boxer punching a speed bag. He was strong and motivated.

Mom immediately stepped in, trying to redirect the behaviors and the physical motions. They appeared violent, at first, then it became apparent that this was the boy's language. She taught me that taking the blows of his jabs wasn't a tolerance of violence, but instead it was her way of listening to him communicate in his language. His actions were expressing his emotions. His arms and legs were doing the work that his voice couldn't. The two gentlemen in front of the boy instantly turned around to see what the commotion was, not yet understanding the complexity of the situation and the language that the child used to speak. As they observed the actions of the child and learned more about his language, their initial frustration at the punching and kicking softened as they showed empathy for both the mother and her son.

As the flight continued, the behaviors seemed to escalate. The kicks and punches became more frequent and more powerful, and the need for movement seemed insuppressible. His body needed to stand up, sit down, look out the window, pull on the seat back and bounce on his seat cushion. With a curiosity so strong and a desire to explore his stimulating environment, he was restricted to one seat and a TV screen as his major forms of entertainment. Not only was this child participating in a day-long traveling event by way of transportation that was foreign, but he was also restricted to a contained space with unfamiliar faces and surroundings.

Mom had one hand in her Mary-Poppins bag almost the entire flight. She grabbed books, an electronic tablet, crayons, and all his favorite snacks; the bottom of the bag seemed endless. She exhausted every activity and every familiar munchy that would help entertain and calm her son, as each item only entertained the child for a few short minutes. In between releases of bursts of energy, the activities, and the snacks, the boy leaned up against my shoulder with little fear of getting closer to a stranger.

How could I be a stranger at this point? I'd been sitting there next to him the entire flight. He reached across me as he had done many times before and opened the window shade. He pointed at the fluffy white clouds and I leaned back in my seat farther so that he would be able to get a better look out the window. I smiled at him and he smiled back at me, then transferred all of his upper body weight to my knees as if he had found a place where he'd breathe in a moment of Zen and allow himself to be hypnotized by the views out the window. The mother tapped her son to try to deter him from continuing to lean on my knees and invade my space. He was in a trance from the clouds passing by.

I looked over at mom and assured her that he was fine—no bother at all. I told her that his leaning on my knees was no different than when my nieces and nephew hung on me to read a book. Having a background in education, I was used to kids testing out the idea of personal space. She cracked a smile of relief and mouthed "thank you." I did notice that she never apologized for her son's actions.

That got me thinking. *Why should she apologize?! I apologize when I've done something wrong or I feel that I may have made a mistake that I should be making a conscious effort to fix. This woman couldn't apologize for her son's actions and nor did I think it was necessary. His actions were how he expressed himself and his intention wasn't to hurt or bother anyone, he was simply communi-*

cating in the only way he knew how. How he communicated wasn't
something she could, or should have to, fix.

The boy bounced around in our seat set only pausing
to throw in a kick or punch, neither with malicious intent.
He leaned over me and played with the window shade. He
had outbursts and then moments of calm. Rotating through
this cycle of activities, the flight continued. His story didn't
end with a witty punchline, a big scene, or emotional tears,
but everyone on that plane did learn an important lesson
that day. Something about being in that moment with the
family opened all our eyes to a larger purpose that we
shared. The purpose became most evident when I thought
about what *hadn't* happened that day.

I hadn't heard one call light go off around us for the entire two hours in flight. I hadn't heard either of the gentlemen in front of us complain once, to either the mother or
the flight attendants, about their seats being punched and
kicked—and they endured a lot of blows. I hadn't seen people shaming the mother for not having "control" and I
hadn't seen anyone calling her to the floor in a way where
she had to defend herself or her son's behavior. I hadn't seen
people judging the boy or describing him using unkind
words. I hadn't heard jabs being made at the family for
choosing to fly with the behaviors the son exhibited. I
hadn't seen judgement; I had only seen acceptance. I had
seen a group of people who had recognized that a child had
different needs than they did and rather than pass judgement and create a more hostile environment, they had
banned together to form a community of support. We all

had offered our little contributions to make each moment a little easier on everyone realizing that it would take a village to help each other get through the flight.

After the flight ended, I couldn't stop thinking about what the rest of that family's day would look like. They had a four-hour flight following the one we flew together. Hopefully, their seatmates would be just as helpful and understanding. Managing the logistics of travel and dealing with cramped seating is daunting enough for any traveler. The mother, however, probably hated air travel for additional reasons. I would venture to say that printing boarding passes and sitting in tight quarters were trivial when considering the overall safety of her child. I had no idea why the family was traveling or where their final destination was, but I was proud of all of them for making the journey and I truly hoped it would be smooth sailing the rest of the way.

Did You Know

The FAA requires that an aircraft be staffed with one flight attendant for every 50 passenger seats available. Even if all the seats aren't full, the flight attendants must be present and accounted for. When considering the flight attendant to passenger ratio, it sheds light on how my mom probably felt when she told my sisters and me, "I'm only one person. You're going to have to be patient."

Lavatory Levers

Some passengers complain that they can't think of a worse seat than one that is near the bathroom. Whether it's the lovely smell, the high quantity of traffic, or the fact that most lavatories are in the very back of the airplane, passengers frown upon seats that put them near the loo. I feel differently. I can't think of a better place to sit where you can be entertained for the entire duration of the flight. Have you ever watched someone attempt to enter the lavatory on an aircraft? Truly, this experience can be a treat.

And what is it about lavatories that immediately causes people to slap on a deer-in-the-headlights look? Many passengers find their way to the lavatories and then they stare at the doors like they've just stumbled upon a secret entrance way. You can see them staring intently as if pushing the wrong side of the door or twisting a handle incorrectly will open a trap door that will eject them from the aircraft.

What you're looking at is simply a door. The worst conse-quence you'll experience for pushing too hard or turning the wrong way is slight embarrassment for not figuring it out on the first try.

The doors don't require a degree in rocket science to be able to operate. In fact, over the course of my career in avi-ation, as well as in the years prior, I've never seen a lavatory that didn't have a short explanation of how to operate the door for entering or exiting. Every single door that I've en-countered had at least one word that would clue the pas-senger in on how to utilize the door properly.

On the day I was working, I observed as a gentleman stopped to look at the lavatory door, which was a bi-fold door that required a push inward to open the door. By sim-ply pushing on the doors, the pressure caused the two pan-els to fold up next to each other inside of the lavatory.

The gentleman stared as many do when arriving at the bathroom. I watched his eyes as he sized up his competi-tion, his eyes bouncing around the frame of the door to de-cide what his first move would be. The bi-fold door had a large crease down the center that if followed to the bottom portion of the door led to two grates allowing a bit of air-flow into the lavatory. At the top of the door were two metal plates, both with the words "PUSH" etched into the metal. Finally, at the level of his waistline was a small compart-ment built into the door with a diagram of a crunched cig-arette on it. None of the components should have been confusing in any way, except perhaps the last component, the ashtray.

All our lavatory doors still have an ashtray built into them. This type of ashtray is very similar to the type of ashtray you would see in a car—made completely of metal, tucked away in the center console where it would snap out when needed and the ashes could be stowed away so as not to blow around the vehicle. Having an ashtray on an airplane may seem antiquated and unnecessary, but if the lavatory doors do not have at least one ashtray attached, the plane won't be allowed to take off.

You're probably thinking, "That doesn't make any sense. This isn't 1967—no one is permitted to smoke on an airplane anymore. Why is an ashtray necessary?" You would be absolutely correct, except for the case when someone hasn't flown in 30 years and he/she fails to take note of the 26 times the cabin crew and the safety demonstrations explain that smoking is prohibited on board all aircraft. That person disregards all warnings and believes that there surely must be a smoking section that exists, like in the lavatory, for example. The passenger lights up a cigarette, and before we land and promptly have authorities meet the flight and the offender, we need a safe place to dispose of the cigarette. The ashtray then becomes very useful.

As I watch passengers like this gentleman eye up the door, I like to give them a moment to figure out the door's functionality all on their own. I'm sure many wouldn't be embarrassed to have the flight attendant give them a tip to simply push the door in to open it, but I'd like to think that unless it's a child, they'll have no problem eventually figuring it out. As the gentleman continued to stare at the door, his hand went straight to the ashtray. He placed his fingertips at the top of it and pulled down the metal plate to reveal the small pocket that was designed to safely extinguish any lit cigarettes. Naturally, opening the ashtray didn't open the door for entry into the restroom, however, he left the ashtray in the current ajar position and took another look at the rest of the door.

Sure enough, the gentleman figured out that he must choose a different action to get the door to open. I thought, *Should I interrupt his turtle-paced game of Bop-It that he began with the lavatory door or should I just let him go?* I decided I'd give him a chance. He saw the engraved metal that read "PUSH" and gently pushed that metal panel to find that the door opened inward. He entered the restroom, locked the door, and used the lavatory. When he was finished, he unlocked the restroom, opened the door, and stepped out. After he stepped out of the restroom and the door closed behind him, he looked back at the door. Staring again, he identified the ashtray that he had pulled open prior to entering the bathroom and pushed the plate back to close it. With the door appearing to be back to the way he had found it originally, he returned to his seat.

I hadn't thought much more about the whole interaction that the gentleman had with the door. At the time, I wasn't shocked to see that he had pulled the ashtray open, because surprisingly many of our passengers will pull on it thinking that they are pulling on a handle that will open the door, just like he did. The only difference in the gentleman's interaction with the door was that he chose to push the ash-tray back into the door panel after he had finished in the restroom. Typically, if passengers pull it out and realize that this action doesn't open the door as they hope it will, they simply leave the ashtray plate in the ajar position and choose not to touch it again. The gentleman, however, did take the time to push the plate back in. Therefore, we'll refer to him as Mr. Ash.

Approximately an hour of flight time passed by, and Mr. Ash returned to the back of the aircraft to use the lava-tory again. I happened to be sitting in the last row of the airplane and while I didn't pay him much attention, I did happen to take a peek at the door while he was inside and noticed that the ashtray had been pulled out and left open again. After using the lavatory, Mr. Ash exited, turned around to face the door, and he pushed the ashtray back so that it would, again, be flush with the door panel. I re-alized at that time that he thought that the ashtray might have served a different purpose than simply being the an-tique ashtray that it was.

After he confidently closed the ashtray and headed back to his seat, I took a moment to decide if I should stop him to explain that he hadn't needed to open and close the ash-tray to be able to enter or exit the bathroom. I figured it would just be a waste of time and because this was his sec-ond time using the lavatory, he would more than likely not have to use it again before deplaning. I was wrong.

The flight ended and we pulled up to the gate. My jumpseat was in the back of the aircraft, so I stood next to the restrooms while I waited as passengers deplaned. Sure enough, Mr. Ash was walking in my direction as he asked, "Hey bud, is it okay if I run in there quickly while I'm waiting to deplane?" I assured him it was no problem, then I gave him very specific instructions, "Please just make sure you give two distinct stomps on the floor before you flush in case maintenance has already begun emptying the tank!" He agreed to follow my instructions.

Before going in, Mr. Ash pulled open the ashtray for the third time, leaving it ajar as he entered the lavatory and locked the door. After finishing up in the restroom, I heard him follow instructions by stomping twice, and then he exited. He completed his routine by shutting the ashtray one last time. Because we were waiting for the passengers to deplane and the gentleman wouldn't be able to return to his seat because the aisle was blocked, I decided to inquire about the new protocol for bathroom entry and also took a second to have a laugh with him. When I served Mr. Ash earlier, I could tell that he was a very pleasant man and he had a great sense of humor. In terms of reading my audience, I knew that he would appreciate a laugh and wouldn't be offended if I made fun of him a bit.

"Looks like we have a few minutes until the aisle clears up. May I ask you a question?" I asked.

"Yeah, sure," he answered.

I pointed to the ashtray located on the door and I asked Mr. Ash if he would please explain to me how the lever worked in conjunction with the door operation. He gave me a questioning look because I could tell that he won-

dered, *Why is the flight attendant asking me about the functionality or inner workings of something related to the aircraft? Isn't
this your domain?*

"What do you mean?" he stuttered with confusion.

"I just mean, you seemed to have a very consistent routine when entering and exiting the restroom. I just happened to notice that you were the only one that used this
lever and I was wondering how it works," I explained.

Mr. Ash was now skeptical and insecure. He hesitantly
outlined his process. "I just pulled that lever out to unlock
the door, so I could push the door in and enter the bathroom. Then, after I left, I pushed it back in to lock the door
into place."

Pretending to understand the explanation he gave, I responded, "Ohhhh! Okay! That makes a lot of sense, now.
You're teaching *me* new things today! I had always thought
that was just an old ashtray built into the door." The gentleman looked at me, and then looked at the picture etched
into the ashtray. He realized that the picture he misconstrued for a door opening was, in actuality, a diagram displaying an extinguished cigarette bent in half. He then
looked back at me to see me smiling at him.

Mr. Ash, laughed at himself and said, "Really? You noticed that I had been opening and closing the ashtray every
time I had entered and exited the bathroom and you didn't
tell me that it was an ashtray?" I admitted that I realized
after the second time he used the lavatory that he thought
the ashtray added some level of functionality. I explained
that I thought he probably wasn't going to use the restroom

again, so I just let it go and smiled to myself. I shared that I was curious what his reasoning was for using that lever, which is why I had to ask him about it.

Still laughing at himself, he added, "I really thought the ashtray was keeping the door in place. I thought it was there so that the door wouldn't slam open or close on anyone while they were going in or coming out. Well, I feel like an idiot."

I tried to help him brush off the embarrassment saying, "Aww, don't feel like an idiot. Those seem like legit reasons for the function of the ashtray. You were trying to keep everyone safe and comfortable. Your intentions were in the right place and I appreciate you for that! So, don't worry — you'd only have to feel like an idiot if you actually stomped twice before you flushed."

We both burst into laughter as he realized that he had just fallen for the stomping prank. He vocalized how ridiculous he thought stomping sounded when I requested that he do so. Luckily, he appreciated my sense of humor and we were both able to laugh at his humorous revelations.

FREQUENTLY ASKED QUESTIONS

What is your biggest pet peeve related to passenger interactions?

Hands down, it's touching and poking. Literally—hands down and stop touching and poking. It is absolutely the most infuriating passenger behavior. Saying "excuse me" almost always works, so why do you have to touch or poke me to get my attention? If I happen to not hear you, then try hitting your call light or waving at me. I'll be right there to help!

Why do we hate being touched, you might ask? Take just a quick moment and think through the entire process of getting from the sliding glass doors of the airport to your seat on the airplane. While you're thinking through that process, also think about every single thing that you touch on that route. Now, think about the sheer quantity of people who have gone through the exact steps and have touched the exact same things that you have. Now go wash your hands, and don't touch me.

Excuse Me

Observing people on airplanes and in airports is what I love to do. While I have no problem diving into a good book or getting caught up in my phone like any other traveler, I can't help but watch as travelers get settled in their seats during the boarding process. Prior to becoming a flight attendant, I was traveling for work and I hadn't had a chance to use the restroom before boarding the airplane, so I dropped my belongings at my seat and ran to use the lavatory. Upon exiting the lavatory, I could see that the aisle was filled with passengers, so there was no sense in trying to swim upstream against the flow of traffic. I stood in the back, out of the flight attendant's way and waited for a clear path to get to my seat. The flight attendant leaned over to me and said, "Smart man! You know better than to try to squeeze past everyone and their luggage. Plus, standing here and watching is like switching on the television. You never know what sitcom you're going to get to watch each day."

What that flight attendant said stuck with me. How many times were funny things going on around me while I was too caught up in my own concerns and agendas that I completely missed them. Think of all the stories that had gone untold for so long because we hadn't been paying attention. I didn't notice anything out of the ordinary standing in the back of the aircraft with the flight attendant that day, but after becoming a flight attendant myself, I eventually came to find out what she was referring to when she said that some days boarding would be like watching a sitcom.

One day, I was traveling for leisure and I had boarded the plane reasonably early. I stowed my roll-aboard in the overhead bin and settled into my seat with my backpack under the seat in front of me. I cleared the aisle quickly. Shortly after I boarded, the rest of the cast of characters appeared. The star of our episode was Ms. Scuseme, who was a middle-aged woman, short and stout, who marched to the beat of her own drum. She didn't mind taking as much time as she needed to get settled, because she hadn't yet noticed that there was a line of people waiting behind her.

Already on the plane were a couple of our supporting characters: Billy Helpful and Miss Outspoken. Billy was a kind-hearted teen, 16 or 17 years old, tall, and lanky. Miss Outspoken was in her early twenties, sassy, and with no time for nonsense. She showed no hesitation in letting others know when she felt something nonsensical was occurring. Our last major player was one of the flight attendants working the flight. He was a patient and accommodating man, always looking to help resolve situations and trying his best to please all passengers with as little conflict as possible.

Our cast was all on-board and while Miss Outspoken, Billy, and I had settled into our seats, Ms. Scuseme and the Flight Attendant were still in the aisle. Ms. Scuseme pulled a roll-aboard behind her: a suitcase larger than one would expect to qualify as a carry-on. I was certain that the bag was not the standard size for a carry-on, but there was always a chance that it would fit — I guess it can't hurt to give it a shot.

Her roll-aboard was specifically the type that had the hard-shelled casing. These suitcases are great travel companions for passengers, but the biggest con is that the width of the bag can't ever be adjusted! With other suitcases, passengers can rearrange some of their belongings in the hopes that the roll-aboard will squish down enough for the bag to be crammed into the overhead bin. With a hard-shelled suitcase, a passenger doesn't have that kind of flexibility. Even if the bag is empty it won't fit in the bin.

Ms. Scuseme attempted to lift her hard-shelled roll-aboard and appeared to be having some trouble. With her short stature as a slight handicap, not only was the weight of her heavy luggage a challenge to lift into the bin, but the hard-shelled bag was likely to not fit simply because of the dimensions. After a failed first attempt, the Flight Attendant noticed that Ms. Scuseme could use some assistance, so he quickly found his way to her seat. "May I help you, ma'am?" he offered.

"EXCUSE ME!" she bellowed.

Her volume and intonation caught the attention of everyone around, and I noticed that the Flight Attendant was taken aback. The look on his face told us that Ms. Scuseme's response seemed unwarranted. The woman screamed those two words in a way that was so abrupt that I was instantly transported back to middle school. I was suddenly hearing the school's retired, crotchety, part-time substitute teacher trying to regain control over her classroom. With all options for quieting students exhausted, the only one left was to scream, "EXCUSE ME!" with a firm tone. While that old crotchety substitute may have had a reason for escalation to this tone, Ms. Scuseme's choice of words and volume were inexplicable.

Realizing that the Flight Attendant was there to help, Ms. Scuseme stepped aside to make room for him to brace for assisting with her bag. Flight attendants have an eye for sizing up bags. They can tell which ones will fit and which ones will need to be checked and stored in the cargo area below before ever attempting to put a bag in the bin. In this case, I was sure the Flight Attendant could tell that the bag wasn't going to fit. From my angle, I knew Ms. Scuseme wasn't going to be successful, because I could see that approximately two inches of her bag didn't have a chance of clearing the top of the bin; the bag was entirely too wide. I've learned as a flight attendant that rather than tell a passenger that a bag won't fit, the best thing to do is to simply help the passenger lift it so there's no questioning whether it will or not. The proof is in the pudding! When the bag doesn't fit, we check it and we're on our way!

The story should have ended there with Ms. Scuseme checking her bag, but she had other plans. By that point, the passengers behind her had waited patiently and had allowed her more than enough time to stow her belongings. The lady directly behind Ms. Scuseme even politely asked if she could slide past to keep the line moving. That passenger was met with the second unjustified, "EXCUSE ME!" The hard-cased bag had been set down onto the seat area while Ms. Scuseme began troubleshooting the issue that already had a simple solution: check the damn bag—it's not going to fit!

Adamant to discover a way that she could maneuver her bag into the overhead bin, Ms. Scuseme decided to start unpacking her belongings. She unzipped the hard-cased suitcase and began pulling out linens and clothes, haphazardly stacking her belongings on her seat and surpassing the height of her seatback. But instead of stepping into the seat set to continue her unpacking, Ms. Scuseme kept herself comfortably posted in the middle of the aisle not giving a hoot that she was continuing to block passengers from boarding. Passengers had been standing in the aisle for a solid 5–7 minutes of the standoff with no end in sight.

Attempting to assist, the Flight Attendant stepped in and said, "Ma'am, would you mind stepping into your row as you work on packing so that those behind you are able to reach their seats?" Well, I'll give you one guess what her response was: Yep, a booming, "EXCUSE ME!" The woman then took her empty suitcase and attempted to try to fit the hard-cased bag into the bin again. I couldn't follow her logic. The Flight Attendant stepped in and told her that her bag wouldn't fit no matter what items she took out of it. Disregarding his expertise, she still demanded that the Flight Attendant help her try to fit her bag into the bin. Shockingly, the bag didn't fit.

Taking a new approach, she requested a plastic bag to put her belongings in. I was not sure what her goal was to resolve this situation. She unpacked her suitcase in the hopes that by lessening the weight of it, she would have a better attempt at trying to fit the suitcase into the overhead bin. A clear disconnect was in play here because the weight of her suitcase wasn't the obstacle to overcome.

After unpacking some of her items, she wanted to take another stab at fitting the suitcase above, but the Flight Attendant was still retrieving the garbage bag that Ms. Scuseme requested for her overflow. Realizing that she needed some assistance, Billy Helpful was nearby and offered to help her lift the suitcase. He was happy to help someone in need, and together they hoisted her suitcase above their heads.

To no one's surprise the unpacking was worthless and the bag still didn't fit into the bin. Except, this time in the attempt to force the bag to fit, one of the wheels of the bag seemed to crumble under the pressure. The wheel completely popped off the bag, soaring through the air and landing in an empty seat set a couple rows ahead. I would be willing to bet that the sheer overpacking and the strain from all the weight in the bag led to the weakened wheels.

Ms. Scuseme, in a rage, stood with her hands on her hips while staring at Billy Helpful ready to give her accusation. "EXCUSE ME! You broke the wheel on my bag, young man! You broke my bag! What are you going to do about fixing it? You're going to buy me a new bag!"

The young man was beside himself. He was embarrassed to now be a character in this woman's absurd performance when his only intention was to offer help to someone in need and to try to assist in moving things along for all the passengers. He was also genuinely sorry that he broke the woman's suitcase. Now she was accusing him of breaking her bag and she was asking for compensation. I thought the poor guy was going to shed a couple tears for being put on the spot with the accusation that sounded like he intentionally broke the wheel.

Stepping in on his behalf was Miss Outspoken. "Ma'am, that boy didn't break your bag. He was trying to help you fit your bag in the bin, which you can't seem to accept needs to be checked! Don't you see it's not going to fit?!" And naturally the response was, "EXCUSE ME!" Were these the only two words in this woman's vocabulary? Ms. Scuseme couldn't help but pursue compensation further, "Young man, you owe me $81 for my suitcase. You have to pay for this suitcase." Before Billy had a chance to reply, Miss Outspoken jumped in again, "Don't you give that woman a cent. You were just trying to help her. It's not your fault that she can't see that by forcing the bag it's going to break it." Then, we were all blessed with another, "EXCUSE ME, mind your own business!"

Miss Outspoken, reacting to yet another abrupt outburst, pleaded "Ma'am, please stop being so loud. I don't
understand why you have to keep screaming 'EXCUSE
ME' at everyone." Ms. Scuseme justified her actions, "I'm
Italian. I can't help it if I'm loud." To which Miss Outspoken snapped back, "I have Italians in my family and they're
nothing like you." I agreed with Miss Outspoken. My entire family is a giant Italian family, and while I understand
being loud, no one in my family continually repeats the
same phrase in contexts where it doesn't make a lick of
sense. Ms. Scuseme seemed to ignore the comment and get
back to the problem at hand. Billy returned to his seat, feeling terrible for being a part in breaking the bag and the
Flight Attendant returned with the garbage bags. He began
helping her to stack her items inside of the bag so that
boarding could finally continue.

By this point the entire plane was frustrated with this
woman. The shenanigans had gone on for at least 15–20
minutes, during which the entire boarding process had been
held up. Those in the front of the plane couldn't understand
why the line wasn't moving, and those in the back of the
plane couldn't understand why Ms. Scuseme wouldn't just
agree to check her bag and get out of the aisle.

Everyone was frustrated and they all had a right to be.
There was no reason why this charade needed to continue.
Miss Outspoken was compelled to address Ms. Scuseme
again, "Ma'am, you have wasted 15 minutes causing a
scene. If I miss my goddamn fucking plane because of
YOU, I'mma be pissed!"

Recognizing that Miss Outspoken had a legitimate concern and agreeing that this had gone on long enough, the Flight Attendant stepped up to address Ms. Scuseme. "Ma'am, we're going to get all of your belongings situated, your suitcase and your bag of items, but we're going to continue this activity in the jetbridge. You'll be able to spread everything out and decide what you want to check with your suitcase and what you'll keep in this plastic bag, but we're taking this outside. We just can't have you blocking the aisle any longer. Please grab your plastic bag."

Ms. Scuseme refused to give up. She demanded that the Flight Attendant help her try to get the bag into the bin again. The Flight Attendant refused and told the woman that she had to check her bag at this point. She agreed to check her bag but demanded that the Flight Attendant get her additional bags to fit the rest of her belongings in so that she would only be checking the empty suitcase. While all the talk of checking the bag was occurring, Ms. Scuseme made a point to let the Flight Attendant know that Billy had broken her bag, but the Flight Attendant seemed less concerned about that state of the bag and more concerned about the disaster Ms. Scuseme created.

The Flight Attendant had had enough of this woman. She wasn't following his directions and he wasn't going to allow it any longer. He gave a head nod that was noticed by the Lead Flight Attendant at the front of the aircraft. The Lead Flight Attendant stepped into the cockpit where she would get their plan of action rolling. Simultaneously, Ms. Scuseme was complaining that no one was helping her to resolve the situation or helping her to try to fit her bag in the bin. The Flight Attendant then told Ms. Scuseme that he would help her pack her belongings in the plastic bags and even carry one of them to the front of the plane, but she should grab her roll-aboard. He was doing everything he could to help her organize her belongings.

The Flight Attendant was able to finally get Ms. Scuseme to step out of the aisle so that the other passengers could sit down. Working together the two packed the plastic bags while everyone else bolted on to find their seats before she attempted to block the aisle again. With most of the plane full, two beefy security guards stopped the boarding process and approached Ms. Scuseme. Relieved and completely misreading the situation she said, "I'm so glad you're here. No one will help me with my bags. I need someone to help me and that kid broke my suitcase." Security told Ms. Scuseme that they needed her to step outside, where they would help her with her bags. As she was escorted off the plane by security, the entire group of passengers began applauding her exit. She might as well have taken a bow.

With the boarding process finally moving along and everyone aware that we were a few minutes behind, the remaining passengers pulled together to quickly find their seats and prepare for takeoff. Then, the door closed. Ms. Scuseme was nowhere to be found. She never returned to her seat. I heard Miss Outspoken express that justice was served, "Good, that's what she gets for causing that mess," and I was sure that sweet Billy was finally breathing easy knowing that he wasn't going to be liable for the broken wheel. Then, I wondered what the conversation with the security guards was like. Do you think their conversation included a lot of "EXCUSE MEs" too?

TRAVEL TIP

Keeping your passport and other important travel documents in a consistent spot for the duration of your travel will help with organization and being sure these documents aren't lost. I also recommend keeping a photocopy of your passport in your luggage in the event that your passport goes missing while abroad. We discourage, however, placing your passport in the seat back pocket. Why? Because once you've shoved the pocket full of dirty tissues, candy bar wrappers, and a half-eaten bag of cheese puffs chances are after you deplane, your passport is getting thrown out with the rest of your garbage.

No Ice

ME: Hello! How are we doing today? May I get you both something to drink?

LADY #1: I'll have a cranberry juice.

LADY #2: I'll have the same, but without ice, please.

ME: Absolutely!

Can you spot the problem with the interaction above? Does anything about the interaction between the two ladies and me sound out of the ordinary? You're probably thinking, *Well, nothing seems strange or out of the ordinary to me! They just seemed to want cranberry juice—sounds reasonable!* That's exactly what I thought as I continued filling orders. I poured the cranberry juice with ice for Lady #1 and one without ice for Lady #2, as requested.

ME: Here we are ladies—one cranberry juice without ice.

LADY #2: Thank you!

ME: ...and a cranberry juice with –

LADY #1, condescendingly and forcefully:— NO ICE! I didn't want ice.

ME, deflated: Oh, okay. All right then.

After seeing how the scene played out, are you able to recognize what we all overlooked in reading the original interaction? That's right! We all forgot to turn on our mind-reading capabilities, because we were supposed to know that Lady #1 didn't want ice in her juice. Pouring an extra drink is never a big deal. Did I end up pouring her another cranberry juice without ice? Of course I did. Did it kill me inside a little to do so? I'd be lying if I said that I wasn't a little bothered by handing over that tepid cup of overly sweet juice to a rude and demanding passenger who probably didn't deserve the extra act of kindness.

What's the big deal? It's just a little bit of ice, I thought. Then, I thought about how that argument could just as easily be used from her vantage point. *What's the big deal? It's just another cup without ice!* So, why was I so frustrated? Pouring one more glass of juice in the grand scheme of the 75–100 glasses of liquid was a drop in the bucket! What's one more?! I *do* hate wasting food and drinks, but in this industry, unfortunately it just happens. But I'm certain that in this situation, wasting a glass of juice wasn't the source of my overall frustration.

Passengers order two drinks all the time and quite honestly, it's no bother at all to pour both. In some instances, the second drink choice is requested as an afterthought and I'm not pressed if I end up throwing away the first one. Fact of the matter is, we serve out of cans and inevitably the beverage service will end with a cart of half-full aluminum cans, holding liquid that will end up going to waste anyway. However, after analyzing the scenario more than I should have, I was able to pinpoint three components of this interaction that drove my lingering frustration.

First, Lady #2 ordered her beverage without ice *after* Lady #1 ordered. The appropriate interaction would have been for Lady #1 to grab my attention and say, "Oh sir, may I also have mine without ice?" Nope, didn't happen. She also watched me add ice to a glass, the second opportunity to amend her order. Finally, she stared at me as I was about to pour the cranberry juice into both glasses. Here's the moment—speak now or forever hold your peace. She. Still. Said. Nothing! She made a conscious choice to wait until after I had poured it to tell me that the drink was preferred sans ice. Seriously?

Secondly, the tone with which Lady #1 said, "NO ICE!" was enough to make me want to pour that entire icy cold cranberry sticky drink all over her head, immediately and unapologetically. "NO ICE!" she firmly said. Those two short words accompanied her look that told me she didn't give a pretzel crumb that I had to make her another drink, nor was she going to take responsibility for requiring a second drink.

I needed to accept that it was obviously my fault for not reading her mind. But, you know, a simple apology or use of manners would have been enough to make me feel like I wasn't her personal servant who was getting his hand slapped for not reading her mind and getting it correct on the first attempt. Oh, and the third reason for my frustration: warm cranberry juice is just plain fucking disgusting and if I worked for the FAA, I would create a regulation against serving it on airplanes.

Customers can sometimes be challenging, but when I look at the bigger picture, the end goal is really just to make sure that the customer is happy, and they leave having had a positive experience. While I still have frustrations that I want to voice, I usually take the route of sharing this type of scenario with my colleagues when we're in the privacy of our own galley, instead of escalating the situation with the passenger.

Some of my coworkers feel differently. Consider an additional scene involving my colleague who felt it was better to handle things a little more head-on. In a completely separate instance on a completely separate flight, I was sharing a cart with one of my colleagues where I was able to watch the reactions associated with her take on a familiar situation.

COLLEAGUE: Hi there, would you care for a beverage off the cart today?

PASSENGER: Can I have apple juice?

COLLEAGUE: Sure thing!

My colleague grabbed a plastic cup, added an appropriate amount of ice to the cup while the passenger watched, and then she popped open the tab on the can of apple juice. She poured the apple juice into the plastic cup and grabbed hold of it, ready for the handoff. Apart from the substitution in the flavor of the juice, the scenario was identical to the one I had experienced with Lady #1. My colleague prepared to hand off the apple juice.

COLLEAGUE: Here's your apple juice!

PASSENGER, pissed: Oh, I didn't *want* ice!

COLLEAGUE: Well let me fill you in on a magic secret about ice: IT MELTS!

My jaw dropped, my colleague unlocked the brake on the cart, and we rolled on to the next set of seats with no regrets. In summary, what can we all learn from these interactions? First, clear and respectful communication is always the best choice. Second, flight attendants have varied solutions to similar problems. And third, warm cranberry juice is still nasty AF.

Did You Know

During warmer months of the year, you'll often see a fog that looks somewhat like smoke billowing in from the vents. The airplane pulls in and tempers the outside air through the air conditioning system. When the air is hot and humid, it creates a water vapor from passing through the air conditioning system. So, there's no need to freak out or hit your call light, just look at it as an opportunity to be a star in your own personal '80s rock music video.

Exit Row Evacuation

With extra legroom comes extra responsibility—in the exit row, that is. Every aircraft has at least one row that is designated as the exit row. Just as it sounds, an exit row is a row of seats that contains a usable exit, either a window or door, for the unlikely event that an evacuation occurs. These seats tend to be some of the most desirable seats on the aircraft because of the amount of extra space to spread out.

What our passengers may not know when choosing an exit row seat is that the flight attendants are required by the FAA to brief every passenger in an exit row prior to departure. Because of the briefing requirement, you'll often see a flight attendant welcoming passengers on board while standing in or near the exit rows. Once all the passengers are present in the rows you will usually hear something that sounds like my personal spiel:

Hello everyone! May I please have your attention for just a quick moment? I'd just like to let you all know that you are sitting in one of our exit rows today. Are you willing and physically able to assist with the window operation in the unlikely event of an emergency? I do need a spoken response from each of you, please.

Then, each passenger must provide some type of spoken answer. A simple "yes" is fine, but brownie points are awarded to passengers who accept the responsibilities with creative responses. Finally, I finish off the briefing by holding up one of the passenger safety information cards that is in the seat pocket so there is no confusion about what information I'd like them to review. I let the passengers know that we'd like them to take a look at the card and if they have any questions or simply don't feel comfortable accepting the responsibilities, they should let us know and we'd be happy to find them a more suitable seat.

The reality is that sitting in this row is a very important responsibility. The questions are in place to keep everyone as safe as possible. Yes, we want passengers to enjoy the extra comfort and legroom, but the point of accepting the responsibilities of sitting in this row is that they are physically able and mentally willing to assist the cabin crew with an efficient evacuation. Over the course of my career, never once has a passenger had to evacuate using emergency exits, but I find it comforting to know that if we would need their help, we would be in good hands. Therefore, I expect that the FAA will continue to require the briefing on every flight.

Keeping in mind that the exit row briefing must be completed before the forward boarding door can be closed, you'll often hear flight attendants scrambling to get the attention of these passengers during the last few moments of boarding. If any of the exit row passengers are the last ones on board, this creates even more urgency to complete the briefing quickly. As was such on this day, I had both exit rows filled except for one seat. I decided that I would brief the 11 passengers who were present and as soon as the last one arrived, I would request an individual briefing.

With just a couple minutes left before the boarding door should have been closed, a gentleman came on the plane to take the last remaining seat in the exit row. He wore a suit and tie, carried a black backpack, and was very interested in continuing a conversation on his cell phone. He was so interested that he was hardly able to give me a few seconds of his attention to verify that he was qualified to sit in the exit row. I had apologized for interrupting him and his phone call, then began rattling off my spiel about sitting in the exit row. Before I even got halfway through my twenty-second briefing, the gentleman interrupted me, "I already told the agent, yes. Yes, it's fine. Yes! Can't you see I'm busy? God!" Then he went straight back to talking on the phone.

I understood that whatever personal phone call he was addressing must have been very important. We transport many business travelers each day and their ability to communicate in between travel and on Wi-Fi while traveling is essential. My briefing took no longer than twenty seconds. It certainly wasn't going to take the entire flight to complete. I was trying to be understanding; it may have been a phone call that sealed a huge business deal. The problem at hand was that the boarding door was closing, and he would need to switch his cellular device to "airplane mode," anyway, meaning he wouldn't be able to continue his conversation.

By this point the Lead Flight Attendant made the formal announcement that as we prepared to push back from the gate, all cell phones needed to be in "airplane mode." Knowing that Mr. Exit Row already displayed very little patience for my first interruption of his phone call, I wasn't very excited to have to approach him again to tell him that he needed to end his phone call. I headed back to the exit row because he seemed nowhere close to the end of his call and he also seemed to be making no attempt to keep his volume down. I politely interjected, "Sir, would you please end your call at this time? Your phone needs to be in 'airplane mode.'"

"Yeah, yeah. Give me a second," he responded.

Typically if a passenger says this, it's followed by something like, "They're telling me I have to get off the phone now," or "The flight attendant is staring at me, I have to hang up." But I wasn't hearing any of those types of phrases come out of Mr. Exit Row's mouth. He continued onto a new topic with the person on the other end of the line and the way he said "Give me a second" was dismissive. The last thing I wanted to deal with was a power struggle where I had to repeatedly tell this guy that he needed to follow the rules; having his phone in "airplane mode" without cellular service was one of those FAA regulations.

I gave him a solid three minutes to wrap up his call after my first request. Then, I approached him again advising, "Sir, your phone needs to be in 'airplane mode' now." He brushed me off and told me that he was hanging up. I wasn't convinced that he would follow through, so I firmly said, "You need to hang up immediately. I'm not going to ask you again."

He quickly snapped back, "Good, I hope you don't!" Then, he continued talking on his phone call.

My middle school teacher reactions had just surfaced. I guess responses like "I'm not going to ask you again" won't ever really leave my muscle memory. While that kind of comment would work with my students because they knew what consequences were in store, I just experienced first-hand how an adult might give zero fucks about that kind of statement. For a moment, I was shocked that he would be so disrespectful and ignore me when I had politely asked him twice to hang up. Part of me was stunned, and all of me was pissed. I certainly wished I hadn't been on the receiving end of his disrespect, but I'll admit, looking back on it now, it does make me laugh. Funny is funny.

At the time I didn't find it very humorous, though. In fact, I was infuriated by the whole thing. I headed back up to the galley and I explained to the Lead Flight Attendant about the interaction I had with Mr. Exit Row. He wasn't complying with my instructions and he was being blatantly disrespectful about it.

The flight deck door was still open and while the pilots were waiting for the clearance to push back from the gate, they overheard our conversation. The Captain chimed in and said, "Hey, is the guy who's giving you a hard time the same guy wearing the navy suit sitting in the exit row?" I confirmed that we were discussing the same person, and the Captain went on, "He's very disrespectful. He was giving the gate agent a very hard time about not receiving a complimentary upgrade because of his frequent flyer status. She was explaining to him that all the seats were sold and had checked-in full, so she didn't have any seat upgrades available to offer him. He was making degrading comments towards her and acted like he had no idea how upgrades worked." After hearing the Captain's input following my anecdote, the Lead Flight Attendant looked at me and said, "Oh really? He's giving everyone a hard time today? Not on my watch!"

My Lead Flight Attendant that day was a woman who had been in the industry for over 40 years. She had seen it all. She was well known within the company. Proof of her popularity lay in the fact that she was friends with the gate agent who was collaborating on the boarding process and she had flown with the Captain several times before. She absolutely loved her job, and after three days of flying together, I could tell that she genuinely took pride in serving passengers and making sure that they enjoyed their flying experience. She was witty with a charming sense of humor, but after what I saw that day, I would never want to cross her.

She stepped into the cockpit and asked the Captain to get the attention of the gate agent and to request that the agent open the boarding door. After voicing my frustration, I went on to tidying up the galley and became distracted by loose ends that needed tied up before we took off. Therefore, I hadn't paid much attention to the fact that the Lead Flight Attendant had a plan of her own. I had just assumed they reopened the door to pass off last-minute paperwork that had been forgotten or recently updated; that type of scenario wasn't uncommon.

The Lead Flight Attendant stepped out into the jetbridge and spoke to the gate agent. I now know that she was explaining the situation regarding Mr. Exit Row to the agent. Not only were they discussing the things that occurred with my interaction, but the agent explained how he treated her during his attempt to fight for an upgrade.

Still out of the loop, I continued working to lock up the galley and prepared for takeoff, then I went out into first class to collect some of the empty cups from the ground service. While I was tidying up, I noticed that the Lead Flight Attendant went out into the aisle and was speaking to Mr. Exit Row who was still on his phone call. She instructed, "Hello sir! Go ahead and grab your belongings. The gate agent is going to upgrade you to your new seat. She just needs you to head up to the gate area quickly so that they can get some information from you."

"Great! It's about time. I had to fight with her forever — I don't know why she didn't give me an upgrade in the first place," he complained. Encouraging him along, the Lead

Flight Attendant added, "She'll take good care of you. Go ahead and walk on up." Mr. Exit Row grabbed his belongings and stepped off the aircraft. The Gate Agent directed him to head up to the podium where he would scan his boarding pass and another agent would meet him to get some additional information.

"Okay then! Just let your Captain know to adjust his passenger count by one in the main cabin. Are you folks all set to close the door?" the gate agent asked. The Lead Flight Attendant assured the agent that she would notify the Captain about the change in the total passenger count and then confirmed that we were all set to depart. I listened as they agreed that it was wonderful to see each other again, then the Lead Flight Attendant thanked the agent for her help and wished her luck with the arrogant exit row passenger.

The door closed and the Lead Flight Attendant continued with her regular pre-takeoff routine as she asked the flight attendants to arm their doors, part of the standard process prior to pushback. Clearly, we were leaving. She stepped into the cockpit and told the pilots that our passenger number decreased by one and that we were ready for departure! She closed the flight deck door and pressed "play" to start the safety demonstration video. We had pushed back, and we were heading to the runway.

I was so shocked that the door was closed, and we were leaving. I tried to form words to understand the situation but all I could muster was, "What happened with the Exit Row guy?"

The Lead Flight Attendant justified her actions. "I told him that we were upgrading his seat so that he wouldn't put up a fight and he would grab his shit and get off. The gate agent sent him up to the podium to get his upgrade," she explained.

My jaw was hanging open in shock. I had to know more! "Oh my God! Did you just leave him behind? Did I just witness the airline ruse of the century?" I asked.

"Honey, I've been doing this since before you were born. I know trouble when I see it. When I went back there, he was *still* on his phone. Trust me, it was the right decision. If he couldn't follow a simple direction to turn his phone off, he certainly wasn't going to follow directions in an emergency, and I just don't have time for that!" she declared.

Laughing in disbelief, I said, "I just . . . I can't believe you told him he was getting an upgrade and then left him behind. I'm speechless. That's kind of hysterical." Winking at me, she defended herself stating, "What?! Where's the ruse? He *is* getting an upgrade . . . it's just not for this flight." I guess she really didn't lie.

Let's face it, none of us should have had to deal with him and he ended up getting what he had coming to him. Still in disbelief, I think I repeated the same sentence probably ten more times throughout the flight. "I just can't believe you told him he was getting an upgrade and then left him behind!"

Travel Tip

What's better than a hot cup of coffee on your early morning flight? When ordering coffee on an airplane, share with your flight attendant what kind of fixings you prefer to craft the perfect cup of coffee. Are you a sugar-and-cream kind of girl? Maybe you're a twelve-sugars-and-four-creamers kind of guy? No judgment! Just let me know how you take your coffee and I would be happy to provide you with all the fixings! Enjoy coffee however you like, so long as I don't have to ask 20 questions to figure out how you take it.

The Impassable Burgers

Y ou may think that some of the most extreme situations occur in the air. Many of them do, but you'd be doing yourself a huge disservice not to tuck away your phone in your pocket during your downtime in the airport. I tend to find that some of the funniest moments I've ever experienced happened before I even stepped foot on a plane, and I'm not sure if it's because I'm ready and waiting to be entertained while I'm killing time or if it's just because I'm a highly observant person. Either way, I've found myself experiencing some of the most interesting scenarios while hanging around many different airports.

In between flights, I like to take advantage of the little downtime that I have to enjoy a meal at my own pace, rather than quickly trying to scarf it down while standing in the galley of the aircraft. One day, I had just over an hour to kill until my next flight, so I weighed my options of restaurants for lunch. I looked around, scoping out a fast food burger joint and a dine-in seafood restaurant. Not having enough time for a dine-in experience and having a seafood allergy, my only viable option narrowed to the burger joint.

After constantly eating in airports, the appeal of burgers and fries dwindled rather rapidly. The length of the line to order overpriced burgers and fries wasn't making this choice any more appealing. Snaking back and forth, heading around the corner from the proscenium of the store front, the queue was making it obvious that not many other options were available for a substantial meal. I will tell you that I was never more grateful that my seafood allergy deterred me from a restaurant than I was that day.

As I waited in line, I noticed that I was quickly progressing forward. What I thought would certainly be at least a 20-minute wait just to give my order couldn't have been more than 10 minutes tops. For the number of people that were waiting in line this was a pretty incredible feat. The workers at this joint were cranking out orders like champions. They appeared to be acclimated to the high volumes of customer orders at peak times and had no problem fulfilling each order. Well, almost no problem.

"Check your burgers! You need to check your burgers!" is what a man was lobbying as he paced the length of the line of customers. *What, exactly, should we all be checking our burgers for?* I thought. *A missing pickle? A chunk of a finger? What?* "There's no burger patties on these buns!" screamed Burgerless Bob. He stomped up to the register ready for a fight.

I recognize that I have more patience than most. I'm not sure if that's because I make my living in a customer service driven industry, but I'm certainly no stranger to overreactions, especially to situations that seem so trivial. I've learned that every story has many sides and if we all exhibit just a smidge of patience, we can usually work together to resolve the problem rationally. Judging by his angry tone, Burgerless Bob wasn't about to participate in anything having to do with rational conversation. All I could do was wait in line and watch this grown man make a complete and utter fool of himself in the middle of an airport restaurant.

Burgerless Bob, or BB, raged, "What are you idiots trying to pull? You think *this* is a burger? There's no meat on the buns! I want my money back! This is ridiculous! I know what you're doing here. You pack up the food thinking people are just going to run away with their bags and not check to see that they're getting what they paid for! Shame on you!"

I had no other reaction than to laugh audibly at this quack while I thought, *Are you serious? Whoa there, BB, pump your brakes for a second. You're irate over a couple burger patties that can easily be replaced. I get it. You order a burger and you expect for it to have a greasy, delicious, beefy patty inside the bun — that's a fair expectation. But if both of my sandwiches were missing the meat, I would just assume that someone made a careless mistake. I mean, come on, look at how fast that line is moving!*

The workers at the restaurant collaborated to function as a well-oiled machine behind the counter and it was inevitable that an order or two would get screwed up. I could totally picture the whole scenario as it was playing out. The cook lined up a bunch of buns, added all the custom toppings and then finished off the sandwich by slapping down the freshly cooked beef patties. She began wrapping up the completed burgers and looked at the screen to anticipate her next move attempting to stay one step ahead, keeping the line steadily moving. Jumping the gun, she accidentally wrapped those two buns having forgotten to place a patty on them!

How does a worker at this restaurant benefit from shorting a customer two burger patties and why would restaurant workers go out of their way to anger their customers who keep the business opened and the employees employed? Instead of being such a jerk, why not just laugh off the situation? Tell the workers that there was a little error made, and then watch as they make two brand new burgers, and maybe even throw in a free order of French fries for the trouble. *Or*, another option for him was to continue being a complete raging douchebag and embarrass himself further. As expected, BB chose the latter.

BB demanded new burgers immediately. The cashier, keeping her cool, assured him that the cooks were putting the new burgers together as they spoke and that his food would be right out. Hoping to expedite BB's exit, the cashier went to get the burgers herself and placed them in a bag so he could be on his way.

Returning with BB's order, the cashier asked, "Sir, would you like to check them and make sure they're exactly how you ordered them before you step away?" He rudely snatched the bag out of her hand saying, "No. They better be right this time. God, a stupid burger place can't even put the meat on the damn bun. How stupid do you have to be to make that kind of error?"

Well, I'll tell you that none of those workers were nearly as stupid as Burgerless Bob. While he was storming off, I inched up to be second in line where I could hear all the conversations taking place behind the counter. I simply observed the reactions of the workers momentarily. I noticed that a cook picked up the controversial burgers and cleared them off the counter to dispose of them. She began giggling. I initially thought that she was thinking back on the situation and just laughing at the absurdity of it all, like I had been triggered with that same bout of giggles in the moment it was happening. Wrong! She saw something else.

The cashier quietly asked, "What's so funny? What happened?" The cook, in shock, responded, "Four. Bites! He. Took. Four. Bites!" The cook showed the cashier the sandwiches and they drew a small crowd of other workers. Truth be told, the rest of the customers closer to the front of the line were just as invested. I, personally, was on the edge of my seat and ready to ask if I could see the buns for myself!

Questioning how this entire scenario could play out, the cook vocalized, "How does it take four adult-sized bites to realize that there wasn't a burger patty on this bun? Didn't he feel how light the sandwich was or take off the top bun after the first bite to see if there was any meat under there?" The cashier, wanting to smile, but ultimately choosing to maintain her poise of professionalism, dismissed her colleague and welcomed me to the counter.

As I approached the cashier, I asked her how she was doing today. She told me she was well and asked me the same question. In response, I said, "I'm really sorry you had to deal with that rude guy. I know what it feels like to have someone speak to you that way when the situation isn't really your fault, and more importantly, when the reason for outrage is so trivial. You didn't deserve to be treated like that. But you carried yourself well—I thought you did a nice job resolving it." Letting her guard down a bit, the cashier told me that it was no big deal but did thank me for acknowledging her professionalism.

I continued, "You know, he probably goes around misdirecting his anger to everyone and I have a good guess why. I would bet that this isn't the first time in his life where he wasn't getting his meat between the buns." That did the trick! The cashier was laughing to herself now. The humor I presented when chatting with complete strangers didn't typically teeter on the line of crudeness, but I just couldn't help myself. He was a dick and he wasn't justified in ruining her day.

We laughed through the ordering process and then I thanked her again for her positive attitude and sense of professionalism. As I handed her my credit card to pay for my meal, she gave me a wink and said, "You're the 1,000th customer today! Your meal is free!" I told her I was happy to pay for my meal and whispered that she didn't have to give me a complimentary one. She just said, "Happy Holidays!"

and I extended my holiday greetings to her, as well. I blew her a kiss as I walked away while both of us were still giggling to ourselves.

Frequently Asked Questions

What is the protocol for serving passengers drinks and snacks if they are sleeping?

Typically, airlines encourage their flight attendants to allow passengers to sleep. Therefore, we won't wake you up to offer you a drink or snack. We respect that your sleep is most important. Depending on the type of service, we may leave items on sleeping passengers' tray tables or an open seat beside them. Other times, usually shorter flights, we pass over the sleepers and let them ring their call lights if they wake up.

While this system works just fine, we do experience the occasional angry, "You skipped me!" First, did I *actually* skip you? Because when I was at your row, your eyes were closed, drool was dribbling out of the corner of your mouth, and your nose was serenading everyone within a three-row radius. So, did I skip you or were you just snoozing? Secondly, I can only think of one extraordinary flight in my entire career where we ran out of complimentary sodas and snacks. There is no shortage of Coke and pretzels on the airplane. Relax, no need to get your seatbelt in a twist. You can have all the peanuts you want!

Tight Connections

Passengers will always have questions about their flights. We expect them to, and they seem to expect that the flight attendants will be able to rattle off the answers at the drop of a hat. "Do you hand out headphones?" "Why don't they start the boarding process with the people sitting in the back of the airplane?" "Is 'A' the aisle seat or the window seat?" "Can I have a blanket?" The list of questions goes on and on, ranging from the simplest requests to some of the most involved queries far above my pay grade. But, by far, the most frequently asked questions all revolve around one topic: connecting flights.

Questions so frequently revolve around connecting flights because some of the passengers can't fathom a re-booking if flights are missed or changes occur to their flight itineraries. Should the flight be delayed by even a few minutes, the number of questions regarding connections increases drastically. While I realize that the idea of missing a flight can be very unsettling, getting worked up and over-reacting certainly won't help the situation. My advice will always remain the same: stay calm and empower yourself to handle the next steps.

Below I provided an outline that I think may be very helpful. I started by sharing three of the most frequently asked questions related to connecting flights. Then, I provided the proper answer passengers can expect to receive as well as an alternative question that might lead to a more productive result than their original question would. And what fun would the outline be if I didn't include the thoughts running through my head when each of the questions is asked.

QUESTION 1: Can you call the gate and tell them I'm coming?

What I'm Thinking

Sure, I'd be happy to call them! Can I borrow your phone that has a cellular signal at an altitude of 35,000 feet? There's got to be a cell tower up in the air here somewhere, right? No, I can't call them. If you scan your boarding pass and it brings up all your information in the computer system, do you really think they don't know who you are and where you're coming from? I know you've heard the announcements before, "This is the final boarding call for Mr. Smith for Flight #555 with service to Boston leaving from Gate

B21." They know to page Mr. Smith specifically because they can see that he hasn't scanned his boarding pass yet. Calling gates is not a thing.

Proper Answer

Our gate agents are top notch, so the agent for your next flight can see that you're arriving on our current flight and will expect you to be coming from our arrival gate. They have your reservation information that is attached to your confirmation code and they know that you're supposed to be making this connection. They will be awaiting you!

Alternative Question

Could you please explain to me the quickest way to get from our arrival gate to my connecting gate?

QUESTION 2: Will they hold my flight for me?

What I'm Thinking

Nope! What? Did you want me to lie to you? Airlines aim for on-time departures. Sometimes that means that passengers on late arriving flights miss on-time departing flights. Would the metro wait for you? How about a bus? I know it sucks to be the person left behind, but can you imagine what air travel would be like if every airline delayed every connecting flight for every person that arrived on a late inbound flight? That would be a hot mess.

Proper Answer

Our gate agents do their best to keep an eye out for all of the last minute passengers and they won't shut that door until exactly 10 minutes prior to departure to be sure they get as many of our passengers on board as possible while still ensuring an on-time departure. You never know, though! Sometimes with the last flight of the night, they'll hold for connecting passengers. Make your best effort to get there as quickly as you can!

Alternative Question

Will the airline automatically rebook me on the next available flight, or do I need to take the initiative to call a representative to make those adjustments?

QUESTION 3: Will I make my connecting flight?

What I'm Thinking

Give me one second while I gaze into my crystal ball. I have no clue if you're going to make your connection! How fast can you run? You booked a ticket where you gave yourself 30 minutes to make a successful connection in one of the world's largest and busiest airports. You must

have believed that you had some magical powers when you booked the flight, so why are you
doubting those powers now? Congratulations.
You just asked my least favorite question of all.

Proper Answer

When you booked your ticket, if the system allowed you to book a close connection, then that
amount of time should be sufficient for making
your connecting flight. Typically, you shouldn't
need any longer than 30 minutes to make it between any two gates in the airport.

Alternative Question

What are my options if I miss my connecting
flight?

I recognize that answering questions about connections
is a necessary part of my job, as annoying as they can seem
at times. Additionally, when passengers are nervous, they
aren't sure what questions they should really be asking. I
think they're just looking to be assured that everything will
work out fine, and I can respect that. The crass thoughts in
my head are a result of the frequency that I end up answering those types of questions, but the truth is, I don't actually
mind answering them.

Questions somehow seem to be the worst when flying
into Atlanta's Hartsfield-Jackson International Airport. Atlanta is known to be the busiest international airport in the
world. The sheer quantity of airplanes that you see flying

into Atlanta is astounding, so any major airline you can think of is more than likely going to be flying in and out of this airport on the regular.

If you've ever been to this airport you know that they have multiple terminals and multiple gates within each terminal. Therefore, making a connection there is almost like being on a treasure hunt. When a passenger asks me how to get from one gate to the next, here is a very real example of the directions that I give:

> *"When you exit the jetbridge into the terminal, you want to go towards the middle of Terminal C where you will find two escalators. Take the escalator down that goes to Gates D, E and F. At the bottom of the escalator is a train that runs regularly in the direction of the gate you need. If the train is there, hop on and take it one stop. If the train isn't there, it will be quicker to walk between the terminals. Once you've gotten off the train at D Gates or you've walked between terminals, head up the escalator. Then, follow signs for the direction of the higher D Gates. Your treasure is hidden under the charging outlet at your gate. Good luck!"*

I'm not kidding when I say that directions get very involved here. I share the complexity of that example to zoom in on the reality of making a connection in Atlanta. So, how can you make this easier on yourself? Whenever possible, the best thing that you can do is give yourself plenty of time.

One afternoon, I was flying from Tampa to Atlanta. Back in Tampa, we had a brief weather delay. Summertime, afternoon thunderstorms are inevitable in Florida and sure enough we were grounded for a short delay of approximately 25 minutes before the storm had passed and we were given clearance to take off. The dangerous winds and lightning ceased and Air Traffic Control called us to the runway. We took off, full speed ahead to Georgia.

In the air, my colleagues and I offered our beverage service. Everything was running smoothly until I hit row 14. At the window sat a woman who was poised. She was a rule-follower, or by-the-book, so to speak. She was an ideal passenger: the type of passenger who only boarded when her boarding group was called, recognized that her purse was considered part of the two-carry-on item limit, and was sure to put her smaller item under the seat in front of her. She fastened her seat belt immediately to not be caught out of FAA compliance, and the consideration of lowering her tray table prior to takeoff was enough to put her nerves through the roof.

While I love this type of passenger on a regular day, flights with any kind of delay completely change the game. When I leaned over to take Ms. By-the-Book's beverage order, I got a little tip that this interaction might end up being a little more than I had bargained for. I asked Ms. By-the-Book if I could get her something to drink. With her order perfectly rehearsed she responded, "Yes, may I please have a ginger ale and pretzels, and I have a question about my connecting flight, too, please. It's important."

While I poured her beverage, I asked a couple follow up questions to see if her concern was something that I had a quick answer for. "Sure! Did you have a specific question about a connecting gate or just a general wondering about a connection policy?" "Well, kinda," she started. "I just wanted to know . . . will I make my connecting flight?"

As I've already stated, this is my least favorite question. The real reason why this question is my least favorite is because I have the snarkiest answers to it and I'll never be permitted to use any of them without negative repercussions. The blurb in "What I'm Thinking" for Question 3 provides just an excerpt of the thoughts that floated around in my mind.

I tucked my snarky responses away for later, and assured her, "I can definitely help you with some of the details of your connecting flight. Just to be sure we get everyone a refreshment before we're required to stow the carts back in the galley, I'm going to work with the other flight attendants to serve everyone the drinks and snacks. Once we get closer to the end of the flight and we have more up-to-date information, I'll stop back here and check in with you to make sure all your questions are answered. Would that be okay for you?"

Disappointedly, Ms. By-the-Book said, "Yes, I guess that's fine." I could tell it wasn't the answer that she wanted to hear. With the few times that I made passes through the cabin to grab supplies I could see that she was looking up at me with a glimmer of hope in her eyes that I might be heading to her row to speak to her and calm her anxiety.

She was one of those passengers that wanted to be told that everything was going to work out just fine.

I certainly wasn't trying to punish her by any means. From my experience with delayed flights, once I begin answering specific questions for each passenger regarding connections, then others will follow suit. This pattern becomes a problem because it slows down the drink service and before we know it, the last six rows of passengers don't receive a beverage or snack when landing is on the horizon.

Additionally, our arrival gate and the connecting gates can change. If I take the time to give passengers their respective connecting gates as well as the "treasure hunt" directions for each of their paths, it might all be for nothing if our arrival gate changes closer to the time of landing. Therefore, we'll see a reduction in stress and an increase in efficiency for everyone involved if we wait until 20–25 minutes out from landing to pass through and talk to the people who have some of the tightest connections.

We finished service while deferring additional connection questions until the end of the flight. As the crew grabbed the trash bags and began collecting, I heard a chime in the cabin and noticed that a call light had been illuminated in the panel above my uptight friend. We were still about 45 minutes away from landing, but I knew exactly what she needed, and if it eased her mind to get the connection information now, then fine.

"Excuse me, sir. Can you speak to me now?" Ms. By-the-Book asked. I told her I would be happy to help but to just allow me a second to pull up the app on my device and refresh it so we would have some real-time updates. Without even processing my request, she barreled through, "I'm going to Phoenix on the flight leaving at 5:10 this evening. I think I was originally going to have 35 minutes to make my connection."

As I caught myself up to speed viewing the updated information in the app I said, "Yes, I see your flight on my list. As of right now, the estimated arrival time into the gate is 4:47 P.M. We're approximately 10 minutes behind schedule. It looks like you'll have a little under 25 minutes to make your connection." Then, repeating my least favorite question, Ms. By-the-Book asked, "Well, do you think I'll make it?"

I have found that the most constructive thing I can do when a passenger asks this question is to give them as much useful information as possible. Remember how in previous stories we discussed people getting frustrated with the lack of control involved with air travel? I think the same idea for anxiousness applies here, because a change in schedule is just another way to lose control over how the day will go. While they have some control over the time the car pulls up to the airport, how smoothly their transitions go through security, and when they board the plane, they don't have much opportunity for input when it comes to the air travel itself.

When a passenger boards that is as disciplined as Ms. By-the-Book was, taking away the ability to control a situation causes her anxiety. The best thing I can do is give her knowledge that will allow her to create a plan that she will have full control over. I explained, "Well, I can't say for sure what's going to happen, but I think the best way for me to help you is to empower you with all the information I can to make catching this tight connection as realistic as possible. Let's start with our arrival gate. As of right now we will be pulling into Gate T5. Your connection to Phoenix is leaving out of D21. Are you familiar with Atlanta's airport?"

By the look on her face, I suspected that Ms. By-the-Book didn't appear to be confident with the layout of ATL. She confirmed my suspicions, "I've been there before but I'm not very familiar with it." I tried to ease her stress a bit and explain as clearly as I could, "I understand. So, you'll want to follow the signs to the escalators that will take you to the train. From there you'll take the train several stops until you get to the D gates. When you get off the train, you'll take a tall escalator to the gate level and then you'll want to follow the signs to D21. If you grab the magazine from your seat pocket, we can peek at the map of the airport and it might help with visualizing my directions."

We took a few moments to look at the map of the Atlanta airport and I repeated those steps again with the visual aid to be sure Ms. By-the-Book had a good sense where she was heading. I even suggested that she write on the map and take it with her as a reference. It couldn't hurt. Concerned about the route I had assigned her, she asked if she would need to take the train or if it would be a long walk.

I explained, "That is quite a hike if you're walking. If you didn't have such a far distance to go between terminals,

I would guess you'd be faster on foot, but because you have to walk between five terminals, the train would ultimately catch up to you at some point. So, you might as well save your breath for a brisk walk once you arrive at the D Gates and let the train do the heavy lifting." Visibly becoming nervous from the instructions provided, Ms. By-the-Book begged, "Well, can I move up closer to the front of the plane so that I can get off right away?"

Unfortunately, I didn't have any open seats any closer than where she was already sitting. I promised that we would make an announcement for those passengers without connections to stay seated so that she and three or four other passengers with tight connections would be able to sneak off the plane first. "Oh great!" she blurted sarcastically, "It's still going to take forever to get off the plane. You're no help! You guys give me 35 minutes to make a connection. That time drops to 23 minutes and it's not my fault that you guys couldn't be on time. I'm not even close to the front of the plane to run off and you offer to do nothing to help me. Shame on you!"

In response I thought, *You're right, ma'am. Shame on me. I went into the skies and started throwing lightning bolts around because I was bored and thought that no one would mind if I conducted my own personal storm real quick. Contrary to popular belief, the airline industry doesn't have any power over the weather. We prefer to fly safely, not through dangerous conditions, but apparently waiting isn't a reasonable solution for you, because you believe that making your 35-minute connection is worth risking people's lives.*

But instead I tried to empathize. "Miss, I'm very sorry there isn't more that I can do to help you in this scenario. Can you think of something within our power that we could do to help you make your connection? I would be happy to do it." Frustrated with the situation and that she was now stumped, she yelled, "I just don't understand why you guys do this to people. This is *your* fault! *You're* making me miss my connection and *you're* choosing not to help me!"

I had exhibited every ounce of patience, had offered help in all the ways I knew how, and showed empathy to her situation. Had she stopped at, "I just don't understand why you guys do this to people," I would have apologized again, walked away, and let her continue wrongfully displacing her anger because she needed to voice her frustration. But now, she was acting like a toddler and was attempting to belittle me in front of the entire airplane when I had done everything that I could to be helpful. She chose to cause a scene by blubbering rude and inaccurate statements for all to hear, so I felt it necessary to clear up one big misconception.

I approached the next segment of our conversation gently. "I'm really sorry that you're upset. May I offer a small recommendation? Contact your travel agency and let them know that you prefer much more time in between your flights, especially when you're connecting in such large airports like this one. Just tell them that this type of short connection just isn't feasible, and it's worse with even a brief delay. It's important that they know they made your travel experience stressful." Barely allowing me to finish my recommendation, she interrupted, "I didn't use a travel agent!"

"Oh, gotcha," I said, understanding that my recommendation didn't apply to her. "Okay, but you had to have called to book with the reservations department. Were you able to let them know that you prefer to sit as close to the front of the plane as possible?" Annoyed that I presented another scenario that wasn't applicable to her, she increased her volume. "I didn't call and book with reservations!"

Playing dumb, I inquired, "So, your travel agency didn't book you and you didn't talk to reservations either? Well wait, who booked your itinerary for you, then?" She was ready to fire back with the exact answer I was looking for. "*I* did! *I* booked the flight." Smiling at her sweetly I snapped back, "Exactly! Have a good day and good luck with your connection to Phoenix!"

The smile was important. I think that it helped me to avoid receiving a bad letter and allowed me to get away with calling her out for her accusations. I couldn't help it. I did my best to help her and she still decided to turn it into a personal attack. We all have our breaking points and I had reached mine. To this day, I have no idea if Ms. By-the-Book made her connecting flight in time, and honestly, I haven't lost any sleep over it. I do, however, hope that she learned how to allow sufficient time between flights when making a proper reservation on her own.

Did You Know

Beverage carts don't have trash cans. Sodas? Yes! Juices? Sure! Trash? No! Think about this: you ordered a drink and right before I went to pour it, I touched someone else's trash. I don't know about you, but if a flight attendant touched someone else's trash right before pouring my drink I would ask him or her to go wash their hands, because that's nasty as hell. I don't need those kinds of germs in my life, and neither do you! This also applies to the people who suck down their beverages so they can place their used cups on top of the cart before the cart moves on to the next row. We have nowhere to put that dirty cup, and what's your damn rush, anyway? This isn't a "Flip Cup" tournament!

Beer Run

My crew and I were working a flight on one of the smaller, simpler jets of our airline's fleet. As strange as this may sound, I've always found something very charming about this type of simpler aircraft. With a lack of in-seat entertainment, passengers engage in activities that aren't quite as common on aircrafts anymore. Usually we see games on tablets, podcasts playing on phones, and movies waiting to be watched. But on this plane, without outlets to juice up electronics, I often see passengers reaching into backpacks to pull out juicy novels, some even aged and yellowed, clearly borrowed from the library. I watch seatmates tentatively offer tidbits about their personal lives, stumbling upon commonalities that develop into networking partnerships and unexpected friendships. And I find passengers sitting with their tray tables down wondering how much longer they'll need to wait before they can purchase a goddamn beer.

Upon completion of the boarding process, I headed to the rear of the aircraft to settle into my jumpseat. I strapped in, latched all the components of my seatbelt, and prepared for takeoff as we taxied on the runway. The back of this aircraft had a unique and cozy setup. Often, inexperienced passengers do not realize what amenities are located here. Some assume that absolutely nothing can be found in the back of the aircraft except maybe an exit door. Others believe that if they head to the rear, they'll stumble upon a five-star restaurant. In reality, if a passenger chose to walk to the back of this plane and pass all other passengers to reach the small cove where I, the flight attendant, sat, the passenger would have three different options, none of which would lead to the surf-and-turf daily special:

Standing in the cove, if the passengers were to turn left, they would see a bi-fold door clearly labeled with a sign that indicates that this door housed one of the lavatories.

If the passengers were to turn right, they would see a bi-fold door clearly labeled with a sign that indicates that this door also housed one of the lavatories.

Finally, if they stared straight ahead, they would see the rear emergency exit. The bottom portion of this emergency exit door had a fold-down jumpseat built into the door exit where I was sitting.

One of the most common complaints from passengers is that they are sitting so far back in the cabin. Um, who purchased your ticket? Many passengers hate sitting in the last row on airplanes, but even more so on this particular aircraft because of its proximity to the restrooms, as described above. The jumpseat, when folded down, is smack between the two lavatories. So, when it is occupied, a more obvious visual couldn't exist that would indicate there is absolutely nowhere to go in this cozy dead-end of the aircraft other than into one of the two lavatories or back to the passengers' seats.

Additionally, if I sat in my jumpseat and a passenger in the last row turned around to look at me, the passenger and I could shake hands since we were no farther than an arm's length away from each other. I mention this to stress that anyone sitting in the last row of the cabin had the same exact view of the rear that I did: two bathrooms and an emergency exit. What you see is what you get. I had no hidden compartments that appeared by pressing a secret button or waving a magical wand. Sorry to disappoint.

At this point during taxiing, the pilots had made an announcement for flight attendants to be seated for takeoff. This announcement served as a clue to the crew that they should be seated in their respective jumpseats, seatbelts fastened, and be prepared for the plane to takeoff. Moving about the cabin at this point could be very dangerous as the flight deck planned to increase the acceleration and lift this bird up into the sky. Makes sense, right? Well, I was unaware, but apparently that announcement was the cue for the gentleman in the last row to hit his call light and discuss his personal requests with me.

As the call light sounded, I looked down the aisle and noticed that the light that had been signaled was, in fact, from the passenger in the last row. Since we were about to take off, I had assumed that this request must have been something urgent. I needed to be sure to keep myself safe, though, so I chose not to release my seatbelt and I simply leaned forward a bit to check in with the passenger. I asked him if everything was okay or if there was an emergency.

The passenger in the last row unbuckled his seat belt and twisted around so that we could casually have a face-to-face while the wheels were rolling and picking up some speed. Completely missing the cue from my comment that perhaps the only request that should have been made at this point should be surrounding an emergency, he asked, "Hey, can I get a beer?"

I paused for a moment because I wasn't sure if he was being serious or if he just had a fun sense of humor. Not after long, I realized he was completely serious. He had no sense of what was happening around him. "Sir, as the Captain just announced, flight attendants have to remain seated at this time. We're about to take off and it's not safe for anyone to be unbuckled or moving around the cabin until we've reached a safe altitude," I advised.

But the passenger in the last row whined, "Bro, can't you just grab one back there where you are, just real quick?"

I thought to myself, *This might come as a shock, but a flight attendant's sole purpose on a plane isn't just to serve you beer.* I'm never offended to be considered a waiter in the sky — serving is the major source of customer interactions and a major component of my job description, but the truth is that almost every additional responsibility and protocol that we have will always take priority over drink orders. While it might be appropriate to get your waiter's attention at a restaurant to immediately kickstart your drinking ventures, that same approach isn't quite paralleled on the airplane. So, I put on a forced smile and did my best to answer his question respectfully.

Withholding snark in this type of situation isn't my strong suit, especially after I've politely given a valid and reasonable justification for not being able to complete the requested task immediately. I looked from side to side of my cozy dead-end of the airplane and asked, "Where, exactly, would you suggest I just grab one from, just real quick?"

The passenger in the last row took a moment. I watched his eye movements as he identified the first lavatory, the second lavatory, and then finally, the emergency exit door-wall hybrid that I was strapped against. No coherent words were uttered, just a low, "Um . . ." I watched him come to the realization that "just grabbing one real quick" wasn't going to happen. So, I instructed, "Please turn around and go ahead and fasten your seatbelt because we're taking off and the last thing I want is an unexpected seatmate in my lap."

He turned around to fasten his belt and then turned his head back to me to say, "I mean, whenever you get a chance would be cool. If it's up front or whatever." I assured him that I would get him a beer when it was time. "Yep. I'll get a chance during beverage service. You know, when we're actually serving drinks and we're not in the middle of taking off."

FREQUENTLY ASKED QUESTIONS

Do people expect you to intervene when babies won't stop crying?

I once had a woman ask me if I would reseat her because sitting next to a crying baby would ruin her entire flying experience. There's nothing worse than a baby or toddler crying inconsolably on an airplane. The parents have nowhere to go, and they've more than likely exhausted all ideas for soothing the wailing child. Dirty looks from fellow passengers don't help the situation. In fact, no one wants the baby to stop crying more than the parents do. In addition to wanting their child's needs to be met, they also would prefer to not be stared at with disdain. One reaction is to utter, "Can you do anything to make that thing stop crying?" but the better option is to ask the flight attendant if you can buy yourself and the struggling parents a glass of wine. Because heaven knows you *all* need it.

The Perfect Storm

As a flight attendant, I know that I have my breaking point with frustrating situations. I know passengers have breaking points just the same. Who doesn't meltdown when enough things go wrong? I find it rare that a passenger doesn't have a justifiable reason for an outburst or display of frustration. The ways that passengers express frustration can vary, but the most fundamental reason for venting the frustration is for empathy. They want someone to recognize that they aren't having the experience that they expected. Since the flight attendants are the face of the company on the airplane, we get to hear all the things that the passengers are upset about.

As an airline, we always aim to meet or exceed the expectations of our passengers, but sometimes for reasons beyond our control, we fall short. The story of Ms. Dynamite is a good example of this. Ms. Dynamite was a middle-aged woman who was generally pleasant upon boarding the flight. I watched her realize that not only was she in the second to last row of seats of the aircraft, but she was also assigned the middle seat. Ouch! That was a double whammy, stuck in the back of the plane and in the middle seat. She accepted both whammies without argument. She took her seat, made peace with the fact that she was sitting in a less than desirable seat, and got herself comfortable.

The flight proceeded as normal, the passengers seemed content and flight attendant duties were accomplished without a hiccup. The beverage service was almost complete as I had arrived at Ms. Dynamite's row. This seat set consisted of a frail elderly woman who sat at the window seat, Ms. Dynamite in the middle seat, and a younger teenager sitting in the aisle seat.

The frail elderly lady was the type of cute older woman who had no clue how to operate anything around her. She had questions about the TV screens, how to recline her seatback, what page the menu was on, where she could get earbuds, and how to adjust her air vent. Learning that the air vent was so high above her head in the panel, she also needed assistance with adjusting that. Ms. Dynamite showed plenty of patience with all the older woman's questions and assisted with her requests.

The teenager on Ms. Dynamite's left made herself quite comfortable by folding one leg under her body so that she was sitting on her left foot and her left shoe was grazing Ms. Dynamite's leg. If that wasn't invasive enough, the teenager's right shoulder slouched into Ms. Dynamite's already limited space. The teen's elbow was supported by the armrest between the two because she had no problem establishing ownership of the armrest for the duration of the flight. When I stopped at their row, each of the ladies ordered sodas and snacks, and began enjoying.

While we were serving the sodas and snacks, I noticed that there was a pungent sewage-type smell that appeared to be prominent in the rear of the aircraft. I recognized that a lavatory wasn't always going to smell like fresh-cut flowers, but the smell was noticeably unpleasant and extraordinarily strong. Sometimes the on-board solutions to nasty odors just don't cut it! I had tried pouring a pot of hot coffee down the toilet with no success. I found the air freshening mist and spritzed several sprays throughout the lavatory and the surrounding area. This was a temporary fix. I even placed an unused coffee bag in one of the lavatory compartments and that didn't seem to be eliminating the odor either.

Later in the flight, we realized that a passenger had discarded used toilet paper in the trash bin instead of flushing it in the commode. Well, that smell wasn't going away any time soon, but when we realized the source of the issue, we locked off the restroom so that passengers wouldn't be able to continue opening the door. But as you can imagine, the smell was problematic for a large portion of the flight until the mystery was solved.

The wonderful fragrance was enough to gross everyone out, but the fun hadn't stopped there. Soon after the beverage service, an exhausted dad walked his infant up and down the length of the center aisle of the aircraft attempting to rock the child to sleep. I think most travelers recognize that babies deserve a "free pass." Babies and young children on an airplane can be challenging and annoying, but the reality is that kids are unpredictable when flying. The whole experience interrupts both the children's and the parents' routines. If something upsets them or they don't get what they want, they're going to cry and throw tantrums just like they would if they were at home.

This day was no exception when the fussy baby in his father's arms couldn't be consoled. The father made every attempt to calm the baby, and while Dad thought he was helping the situation by walking the length of the plane with the child, he was actually subjecting each and every passenger to an equal opportunity to hear the wails of his son. Everyone felt bad for both the child and the parents, but no one would have been upset if the child fell asleep. And, honestly, no one wanted to be the one stuck next to the screaming kid. Dad decided to post up in the rear of the aircraft, near the stinky lavatories. His spot was next to the row where Ms. Dynamite was being elbowed by a teen with no sense for personal space and was bombarded with requests from a needy, elderly woman.

After realizing that standing in the back wasn't helping the child get to sleep, Dad eventually continued his stroll and gave those in the rear of the aircraft some reprieve. But regardless of his location in the airplane, the baby's screams echoed. Was it possible that the situation would get worse for Ms. Dynamite? What's worse than two invasive seatmates and a screaming child?

Well, it absolutely was possible for things to become worse. I took a lap up and down the aisle to collect trash that remained from the beverage service. As I arrived upon Ms. Dynamite's row, she seemed rattled. Who could blame her with all her fellow passengers giving her the experience of a lifetime?

I began chatting with the three ladies in the row. "Anything you'd like to discard? May I take anything out of the way for you?" I saw that the elderly woman at the window had a nearly full cup of Coke sitting on her tray table. She reached for it as she was telling me that she didn't care to drink anymore. She lifted the glass and instead of asking for assistance, she raised her arm to pass it off to me with what seemed like a push in my direction as if it would float on its own. Truly, this handoff was almost like a toss, because I believe that the little old woman didn't have the strength to hold the weight of the cup up in the air. She must have thought that I was closer to grab hold or that maybe I was able to catch it. Unfortunately, my hand was nowhere near the glass and nor did I know she was about to toss it in my direction to try to throw the liquid away.

The entire cup, which held the contents of half of a can of Coke, landed in poor Ms. Dynamite's lap. She was completely soaked from the full, lukewarm cup of cola. Strangely, the liquid only landed on Ms. Dynamite. It covered her pants and her blouse, dripped into her purse, and splashed onto her boots. Both the elderly woman and the teenager seemed unscathed by the soda explosion. In fact, the elderly woman simply turned to face the window as if she played no part in any aspect of this spillage, and the teenager went back to her movie as soon as she verified that her clothes hadn't been soiled with any of the sticky soda. I ran to the galley immediately to grab some towels to help her clean up. I felt bad that she had been spilled on and I wanted to see if there was anything else I could do to help.

"I'm so sorry that drink was dropped on you," I apologized to Ms. Dynamite. She agreed that she was sorry it happened also and then informed me that she still had another three-hour flight to take after this one. She was frustrated because she was going to be all wet and sticky for the rest of her day.

I apologized again and offered her a couple towels with warm water to clean her hands, and I also had dry towels to soak up any leftover soda. The last set of towels had club soda on them to help pull out some of the Coke on her clothes. I couldn't stop apologizing and instinctively spouted another "I'm so sorry."

"It's FINE. It's not your fault," she yelled out of frustration. I collected the used items as she finished with each set of towels. She seemed to keep her cool until the moment that she realized the soda had spilled into her purse that was sitting on the floor. The spill didn't end there—the soda splashed onto her suede boots and she was finally realizing it. Escalating from the realizations, she complained, "Oh no! It's in my purse! Aw, really?! Ohhh, and it's on my boots, too?! They're going to be ruined. Damn, I just bought these!"

Her frustration just kept building and I couldn't think of any other way to help except to keep providing her with a variety of wet and dry towels that she used to clean up the mess. At that point thoughts started streaming through my mind. While I certainly wasn't as annoyed as Ms. Dynamite, I was bothered by the fact that the elderly woman had pinned the spill on me, taking no responsibility for her role in the disaster, and hadn't once apologized to Ms. Dynamite. Maybe she truly hadn't realized that it was her fault, but she certainly found a quick way to appear distant from the whole scenario.

At the other end of the seat set, the teenager was acting as if nothing had happened around her. She hadn't stood up or made any extra room for Ms. Dynamite to clear the soda away. She couldn't be bothered to even pause her movie, let alone offer to help clean up or hold anything to make this situation a little easier for her seatmate. I was feeling frustrated for Ms. Dynamite, but I was also nervous because that was the first time I had ever spilled a drink on a passenger and it wasn't even really my fault. All I could think to do was apologize to her excessively. I felt terrible about it. That was probably the wrong move.

"I'm really, really sorry this happened. What else can I get you that would help?" I offered. She declined any other assistance but was obviously still frustrated. Feeling her frustration, I continued, "I'm so sorry, miss. Are you sure there isn't anything I can do to help you?" My apologies just exacerbated the problem, and we weren't getting anywhere.

Ms. Dynamite, finally exploding, explained, "I'm covered in Coke, it smells like shit, and that baby won't shut the fuck up. I'm ready to get off this plane."

I felt terrible as she pointed out each reason for the worst flight experience ever, yet I couldn't help but laugh at the blunt reaction Ms. Dynamite had; she definitely hit her breaking point and the way she exploded was kind of hysterical. I couldn't do anything to fix any of her problems, aside from the attempts I had already made. I didn't even have another open seat for Ms. Dynamite to escape her sticky situation.

I have had days like that, whether in the air or on the ground, when a string of unfortunate events took place and there was nothing anyone could do to make any of them better. I recognized that no matter how much I wanted to try to help fix the situation, my best bet would be to just give her some space. I just wished there would have been something else I could have done. Unfortunately, Ms. Dynamite bolted off the plane that day, and she wasn't a very happy camper. I couldn't blame her.

The reality is that any of us could be a Ms. Dynamite. Hell, maybe you already have been. I'd be lying if I said I never wanted to cuss out another passenger myself. You can be sure I've considered the option of telling the guy next to me on a flight to get his damn elbow out of my side. But what I'm trying to say is that the frustrations we all experience stem not only from any unpleasant encounters with each other, but from the fact that there isn't much any of us can do to have more control over the cramped environment that we're in when we fly. We're all human and we make mistakes — an accident is an accident.

While Ms. Dynamite's bold explosion was funny, it helped me recognize that we all share those frustrations and we can all be more considerate of our fellow travelers. Let's agree to help each other, because when it rains, it pours, and sometimes when it pours, it's Coke . . . all over your good boots.

TRAVEL TIP

Never forget that your flight attendants are always there to help you. Aside from being ready to step in during the unlikely event of an emergency, we're happy to help you with any questions or special requests. You want a mimosa? Ring the call light! It's not a problem! You want a mimosa with one-third of the single-serving bottle of champagne, a separate glass of orange juice, and a separate glass of ice? Ring the call light! You got it! You want to continue this cycle of ordering complicatedly served mimosas eight more times? You know the drill. I can't promise your seatmate won't break your finger off after reaching for the call light that many times, but I can promise that I'll bring you exactly what you want every time with a smile, or at least some fake version of one.

Cancun Chaos

Many people ask if flight attendants ever experience any crazy things on vacation flights. When it comes to working a Cancun flight, the question isn't really *if* you'll experience a crazy event or request, but *when* you'll experience a crazy event or request. And really, a better phrasing would substitute "when" with "how many" crazy events and requests you'll experience in your day. Something about a vacation destination always leads to a memorable day at work.

This flight to Cancun was no exception. The whirlwind boarding process started with a gentleman, Mr. 18D, who probably kicked off his morning at an airport bar and chose to pair his eggs and bacon with a couple of Bloody Marys. We could all tell that he was having a good time, was in great spirits, and had certainly entered vacation mode even before stepping onto the plane. His voice was a bit louder than expected, or preferred, for a flight that boarded at 6:30

AM, but I don't know that I would have pegged him to be intoxicated … yet. Boarding continued and I floated through the cabin to help passengers get their belongings stowed and locate their seats.

While I was passing through the cabin, a call light illuminated, and I heard the ding. Ms. 36F was trying to get a flight attendant's attention. I made my way to her seat section and asked if there was something that I could help with. "Yes. I'm trying to blow up my neck pillow and I just don't have the breath to do the whole thing. I'm getting tired. Would you please finish blowing it up for me?" requested Ms. 36F.

The woman had attempted to inflate her neck pillow and had been successful with approximately one-third of the air required to fill the pillow. I wished someone had a photo of my face when she asked this. I calmly explained, "Ma'am, I'd like you to take a second to put yourself in my shoes. If I had asked you to put your mouth on the nozzle of my neck pillow to inflate it for me *after* I had already put my mouth on the nozzle, would you be willing to help me?"

She told me that she "got it" and I continued, "Sorry, but it's going to be a hard 'no' for me. That wouldn't be sanitary or safe for us to help with things like that. Are you traveling with anyone around you that wouldn't mind helping you?"

Regretfully, she responded, "No, unfortunately. I'm flying by myself."

If she really thought that asking a stranger to help her blow up a neck pillow that she had already slobbered all over was a reasonable request, then maybe she shouldn't have been traveling alone. Just saying. "Well, I don't know if this helps, but I've always found that if you bite the nozzle while simultaneously blowing, the inflatables seem to fill quicker," I suggested.

"Well, do you have a pump I can use?" she asked. I raised one eyebrow and gave her a look as to say, "Did you seriously ask for a frickin' pump?" As she realized that I thought she was crazy, she added, "You know — something you'd use to inflate a raft!" I thought, *Sure, ma'am, let me just go back into our Phys Ed closet where we keep the soccer balls and spare bikes. I'm sure the tire pump's in there somewhere!*

"No, ma'am, that's a negative. We don't have any pumps on board," I said, being the bearer of bad news.

Shocked to hear of the lack of pumps, she raged, "Well, we're about to fly over a lot of water. How do you all plan to inflate the rafts in time if we need to escape?"

I thought for a second how I wanted to handle this. *Should I make a joke out of this to poke fun at her so we could all have a giggle? Would she be offended? After asking me to help blow up the pillow, requesting a pump, and asking how we would inflate the rafts in time, I somehow thought that my joke would end up being lost on her.* With our previous conversation in mind, I decided to just stick to the facts.

"Ma'am, in the event of an over-water evacuation, all the life rafts are equipped with a system that uses compressed gas to rapidly inflate the rafts. I can assure you that no one will be using their lungs, or a tire pump, to inflate rafts if there's an emergency," I said calming her concerns.

Thinking through the process, Ms. 36F dove into hypothetical questions. "Out of curiosity, what happens if they don't inflate?"

Knowing that these questions sometimes stem from anxiety and fear, I decided to keep my answer light, yet factual. "Well, you would also have an inflatable life vest on. So, if that happens, you and I are going to get ourselves out of this airplane as fast as we can, and then we'll float lazy-river style the rest of the way to Mexico together. How does that sound?"

Finally catching on to my joke, Ms. 36F said playfully, "As long as you're bringing the beer, I'm in!" I smiled at her and told her that I liked the way she thought. With that fire extinguished, I turned my focus to closing some bins and checking in with the rest of the passengers as we wrapped up the boarding process.

I had finished with 36F just in time for 15B to ring his call light. As I walked to the front of the cabin to attend to the next call light, I passed by row 18 where my boisterous friend from boarding was cackling with his crew. He still wasn't using a volume appropriate for the hour of the morning or his "indoor" location. But ignoring 18D for now, I approached 15B.

I found a gentleman in his forties traveling with his family and ready to ask me a question. "Hello sir. I was wondering: Am I permitted to take my shoes off during the flight?"

Keeping a straight face, but obviously kidding with him, I stated, "No, sir. You must keep your shoes on the entire flight. The FAA mandates that any passenger caught without shoes must be ejected from the aircraft, even if midair. There is a sensor under the seat in front of you that detects foot odor."

That was not the answer he was expecting, and he hadn't yet picked up on my joking tone. He started to explain to me that he had some sort of burns on his feet and it would really be painful to keep his feet in his shoes for such a long period of time. I started laughing at him, mostly because he was taking me too seriously, and said, "Sir, I'm kidding. That was a joke. No one is going to eject you from the plane if you take your shoes off. As long as your family doesn't mind, then it's fine with me."

Then, I directed my next question to his young daughter. "What do you think? Are Dad's feet stinky? Should he keep his shoes on?"

She had no qualms throwing him under the bus. "Daddy, your feet are the stinkiest!"

I told the gentleman that I didn't think an ejection from the FAA was what he needed to worry about. His daughter seemed to be the tougher critic!

I explained to all the members of the family that ejection is not a thing, and I was only joking. I assured them they wouldn't get booted, shoes or no shoes, and all was well. Questions seemed to be answered and concerns addressed. The safety demonstration had played through, the final safety checks had been completed, and then it was time to take off. The lead flight attendant and I took our jumpseats in the front of the cabin and strapped in for takeoff. The way our seats were situated presented me in a rear-facing jumpseat at the front of the aircraft. Therefore, my jumpseat allowed me to look straight down the center aisle where I saw all the passengers. My colleague, however, was to my right and her view of the cabin was blocked by a thin wall with emergency equipment securely mounted to it.

We had taxied to the runway and the aircraft was aligned for takeoff. Just when I thought we had gotten all the crazy requests and situations out of the way during boarding, the plane tilted back, we lifted off toward the sky and a passenger gave a thrilling yell. I looked out into the aisle and then back at the Lead Flight Attendant in disbelief.

Mr. 18D was screaming at the top of his lungs, "WHEEEEEE!" The Lead Flight Attendant immediately looked to me to ask, "What was that?!" I started laughing and told her that I really wished that she could see what I was seeing. Getting nervous for what I was about to share with her, the Lead Flight Attendant inquired, "Is everything okay? What's wrong? Do I need to call the pilots?"

"No! Everything is fine . . . kinda," I said attempting to ease her concern. "Remember that guy who was pretty loud when he was boarding—we thought maybe he had a couple drinks in the airport? He's sitting in 18D." She recalled the passenger I was speaking of and then begged to know what he was doing. "He has his arms spread out across everyone like airplane wings, while screaming 'WHEE!' at the top of his lungs."

"No more alcohol for him. He's cut off!" demanded the Lead Flight Attendant. *Wow*, I thought, *cut off before he even started! That's an accomplishment!* I saw that 18D was having a great time. The entire rest of the cabin sitting in front of him whipped their heads backwards to see who was causing such a commotion. Most of them laughed, realizing a grown man had decided to reenact a five-year-old's take on "airplane," while the rest rolled their eyes. Fortunately, after take-off, Mr. Airplane responded positively to a friendly chat with the Lead Flight Attendant and ended up being on his best behavior, choosing to sleep through most of the remainder of the flight.

Other passengers, not so much! The beverage service started, and I served the passengers up to row 27. In this row sat a group of young women in their thirties who were ready to celebrate vacation! They were all smiles, excited for a holiday, and probably had consumed one or two drinks in the airport. They all seemed to have playful senses of humor. They joked with and about each other, then even let me in on the jokes, too. I asked them what I could get them to drink. The woman in 27C answered for the group, "We'll each have a vodka-soda, with lime." I used my device to ring up the sale for three bottles of vodka, told the ladies that I would pour those drinks for them, and I returned to the beverage cart to grab a miniature bottle of alcohol and a glass of soda water for each of them.

All the alcohol, including the bottles of vodka for the three drinks requested, were housed in the lowest drawer of the beverage cart. Naturally, collecting the three bottles from the low shelf would require that I bend over. Prior to working my first flight, I had been advised by my trainers and colleagues that when bending over in the aisle, I should always bend at my knees and avoid bending at the waist to grab items from the cart. My colleagues shared horror stories of how they had bent at the waist in the past and terrible things happened.

One colleague shared that her pants split right down the seam, and she couldn't think of a moment more embarrassing that had happened to her in front of passengers. Another mentioned passing gas, and I'm still not sure I believe that happened, but I guess it's possible. Either way, both scenarios would have been avoided if they hadn't bent at their waists while on the cart. The moral of the stories: bending at the waist opens the door of opportunity for a lot of bad things to happen.

Having this knowledge in the back of my mind, I've always bent at the knees to squat low enough to access the liquor drawer. Except, today! As I went to bend down, the flight attendant on the other side of the cart asked me a question. Attempting to keep my head up high enough for my voice to carry to her while simultaneously allowing myself to reach the bottles of vodka, I ended up bending at the waist. I had just committed the cardinal sin of flight attendant beverage cart serving. I was immediately forced into repenting for my sin, by way of 27C's great sense of humor. Having had a couple drinks in her system, she unintentionally taught me an important lesson that day.

While I was mid-bend, my butt ended up right at her eye level. I don't know if it was because she was surrounded by the great group of friends, that I had built a rapport with all of them, or the one or two glasses of liquid confidence she had consumed before boarding, but she was obviously much less inhibited. Who knows, maybe it was a combination of all three that led to what would happen next.

I envisioned that she tapped her three friends to let them in on the joke that she was about to make. As I was standing one row behind her and she was still facing forward, she moved her forearm and hand forward to allow for space to then swing her hand backwards. The entire motion was done as a joke to pretend to slap me right in the butt, as it sat idle right at her eye level while I collected the bottles of vodka. The only problem was her spatial reasoning skills were a bit off. Maybe it was the alcohol or maybe it was the fact that I was a moving target, finishing the bend at the waist, but she slapped me square in my ass and everyone in the two rows I was serving gasped, myself included.

I thought it through for a brief second. First, I realized that the whole situation could have been avoided if I hadn't bent over at the waist like everyone had warned me. Second, was it really intentional? Did she mean to deliberately whack my butt or was it an accident? While I don't ever condone any type of sexual objectification, something about this scenario seemed like a genuine mistake—a gag that went very, very wrong. I had two options planned to handle this situation. If she was being deliberately offensive, then I'd take a serious approach, but based on the relationship I had established with her and her friends, I hadn't perceived any maliciousness. Therefore, I was fully prepared to go with a less serious approach.

I put on a very stoic face—one that displayed my best impression of my third-grade teacher when she knew that I knew that she knew I did something I shouldn't have. That look that said, "Is there something you'd like to say to me?" She was as white as a ghost. Her friends next to her and the passengers across the aisle had their bulging eyes glued on me, awaiting my reaction. Essentially, Miss 27C had "assaulted" a flight attendant for no good reason and this situation could have potentially had a very serious consequence.

I stared at her, seeing the anxiousness and fear all over her face, awaiting to hear how she would justify the whack. She couldn't get her apology out fast enough, "Oh. My. God. I am sooo sorry. I was just joking. Your butt was just right there, and I just wanted to *pretend* to hit it, but then I actually *did* hit it. I didn't mean to hit you. I really didn't! I'm mortified. Oh my god, I'm so so sorry! Please forgive me!"

By that point, she was trying to remain as sincere as possible, but I could tell she felt so ridiculous for having to apologize for something so awkward that interruptions of nervous laughter hiccupped through her apology. I took my time, being sure not to let up my expressionless face, and I said, "I really am at a loss for words. I can't believe you. I charged you for three vodkas. What you just did was not included in that price—booty slaps cost extra." Then adding in a whisper, "Cash only!"

Finally breathing again, 27C laughed a sigh of relief. She continued to apologize profusely and explain that she hadn't intended to hit me or embarrass me in front of everyone. I assured her everything was fine and that I knew it was an accident. Before someone jumped on the WI-FI and sent a letter into the company about the "extra" services I shared that I could provide, I cleared up my joke with the passengers. I explained that she was the only passenger to ever hit my butt and honestly, I thought it was funny especially because she hadn't intended to follow through with the whack.

Rather than make a big deal of it, I thought it was more appropriate to make light of it. They all laughed and agreed. To this day, I thank that lady in 27C for teaching me the lesson that I should never bend at the waist by way of colorful, on-the-job training that I never thought would be part of the job description.

Did You Know

Flight attendants must remain seated and strapped into their jumpseats any time the plane is taxiing. Exceptions can be made for safety-related duties only. If a flight attendant puts one of your requests on hold until the aircraft reaches a cruising altitude, don't be offended or chalk it up to poor service. We just don't want to be personally fined by the FAA for breaking an important regulation. So, while wanting to start that movie you've been dying to watch might seem like an emergency, offering earbuds doesn't quite qualify as a safety precaution.

What's the Hold Up?

After finishing a full day of flying, I thought I would take my chances running to catch a last-minute flight back to my hometown to spend a few days off visiting with my family. When flying on a flight for leisure, I have the option of waiting as a standby passenger in hopes that a passenger seat will be available, or I can book one of the extra flight attendant jumpseats as a way to guarantee that I will have a promised seat on a specific flight. Seeing that the jumpseat was still available, I snatched it and checked in with the gate agent.

When booking this type of seat, I typically board the plane early and get settled, introducing myself to the rest of the working crew and stepping aside to wait as the passengers board the aircraft. Today was like any other. I boarded early, waiting at the back of the plane for the boarding process to continue and for all the passengers on standby to receive the seat assignments they were patiently awaiting. Now that all the passengers were seated and the standby passengers had trickled aboard, I was given the okay from the working crew members that all passengers were on board and I could choose any of the remaining seats that were available.

The crew informed me that a window seat was available toward the front of the aircraft, so I strolled forward to scope out the situation, hoping to sneak into the coveted seat before someone else moved to it. Awesome, there it was! Still available was my upright bed for the next two hours. I recognized that by taking this seat I was also crushing the dreams of my seatmates who were praying to the airline gods that the seat would remain empty and they could both spread out a bit. "Sorry, friends," I said. I treaded lightly, extending an apology to the two gentlemen currently sitting in the row, one sitting in the aisle seat and another in the middle seat, as I attempted to occupy my seat at the window.

Politely asking permission to enter, I said, "Excuse me folks, so sorry to bother you. May I please slide in your row to the window?" With an unexpected gruff tone, the gentleman on the aisle said aggressively, "What?! What's going on?" In his defense, I was in my complete flight attendant uniform, having just finished a working trip. Naturally, if I were a passenger, I would have been confused and thought it strange that a flight attendant who appeared to be part of the working crew was now asking to climb into a row and grab a passenger seat.

In response to his aggressiveness, I kept it light. "I know, I probably look like I'm going to be serving you on this flight but I'm actually off duty and I'm just commuting home to see my family. I'm going to be sitting in that window seat if I could please just sneak by you gentlemen." The passenger on the aisle couldn't care less about my explanation. He just gave me a look of disgust and told me to just slip by.

Mr. Aisle did not stand up or make even the slightest attempt to move out of the way. He side-saddled his legs as his non-verbal cue signaling me to go around. As a result, the poor gentleman in the middle seat was given no option to stand up or move to the side because his seatmate at the aisle had made it clear that he wouldn't be bothered to budge and make this transition easier for anyone involved. I crossed my fingers and hoped that no portion of my bag or body would brush against the curmudgeon on the aisle. I instantly felt terrible for the gentleman in the middle, as I had no option but to use him as a crutch so that I didn't tumble over and crush them both.

Luckily, I cleared the two gentlemen, rolled my eyes at the ridiculousness of the situation and then I extended a genuine hybrid apology/thank-you to the passenger in the middle seat for invading his personal space and for helping me keep my balance. He didn't seem to be bothered by what most would expect as part of the public transportation experience—people are actually going to fill the empty seats.

While continuing to smile I settled into my seat, but I noticed that some of the other passengers were trying to catch my attention, directing serious side-eye toward Mr.

Aisle as to say, *What's his problem?* or *What a jerk?!* due to his extreme reactions to a simple request.

By this point in the day I had been flying for 13 hours and I was ready to focus on unwinding. I stowed my bag under the seat, plugged my phone charger into the seat's outlet, secured my headphones and began my plan to avoid attracting any additional attention or drama for the remainder of the flight. I was hoping to get a solid nap in during the flight.

Settled in my seat, I peeked at the time on my phone. I noticed that the flight happened to board up very quickly and all passengers were sitting on the aircraft as the baggage handlers finished loading cargo and the caterers loaded all the provisions necessary for the flight. Our scheduled departure time was five minutes away and everything seemed to be running smoothly. We were right on schedule when Mr. Aisle began tapping me, which I despise. Then, he asked, "Hey! Hey! What are we sitting here for?"

I took a quick moment to send a "thank you" out to the universe for giving me the patience to dig deep, muster up some sense of decorum, and continue showing kindness to this bundle of nerves, while I was momentarily seeing red in reaction to being touched by someone I didn't know.

"Well, sir, I can see out the window that the baggage handlers are finishing the loading process and catering seems to be buttoning up everything in the back galley, so when they're done we should be on our way," I shared.

In what seemed like a threatening tone, Mr. Aisle demanded, "Well, we better leave on time!"

I didn't recall ever claiming to have any kind of control over what time this flight would leave. Paying him no mind, I turned away and replied, "Mmmk." I could tell that everyone around me had also had enough of Mr. Aisle already and, sadly, we hadn't even closed the boarding door yet. The passengers behind me unified in a chorus of teeth-sucking as at least two other people joined in sharing a vocalized agreement of annoyance for his loud, dramatic comments.

The plane was ready to push back, and we began taxiing to the runway. The taxi took approximately 15 minutes and then we remained idle for another four or five minutes, awaiting take off. I could see from my window that we were in line for our turn to take off while Air Traffic Control was coordinating the runway usage simultaneously for aircrafts that were landing. This was a standard process at any time of day, but especially during peak flying times.

This time of night was comparable to rush hour traffic on a freeway. Many planes were coming and going, and every aircraft had to take its turn. Believe it or not, all airlines are aware of these high-traffic times and they pad the published flight times with a buffer to account for the extra time it may take for taxiing. They do this to ensure the aircraft still arrives on time. Aisle didn't seem to understand this and felt the need to voice his frustrations rooted in impatience. Flailing his arms and fiercely tapping his watch, he yelled, "Jesus Christ! What's the hold up?"

"They're waiting for you to shut the fuck up! Just relax for God's sake. You're driving everyone crazy. Chill, bro!" a random man yelled from the back of the plane. The random man mimicked the teenage boy that we all had sitting in the back of our Social Studies classes, never scared to chime in with his two cents, especially if his comment would earn a laugh. I had never been so happy to be tucked away in my window seat so that I could laugh into my shoulder and enjoy one of those satisfying moments where a passenger served up all of the sass-filled clapback that I thought in my head, but chose not to say for the sake of professionalism. Hearing the general laughter from Random Man's response, Mr. Aisle realized that he had pissed off the people sitting in the surrounding rows, so he finally shut his mouth and relaxed for takeoff and the rest of the flight.

Travel Tip

Hi! Hello! Good morning! Hey! Good day! Good afternoon! How are you? How's your day? How are things going today? Having a good day? Happy to see you! You can say literally ANYTHING, but please just say SOMETHING when a flight attendant welcomes you aboard the aircraft. Responding gives both of us a quick moment to get to know one another and might even help us learn ways we can be of more assistance to you. But, strangely enough, completely ignoring our existence doesn't give us the warm and fuzzies like you might think.

The Republic of Los Cabos

Wintertime: the temperatures are dropping, the snow is falling, and the air is crisp and clean. Passengers pull up to the airport curb in their cars, excitedly bouncing out of their vehicles and unloading their roll-aboards, duffle bags, backpacks, and floppy pillows they snatched from their beds in a flurry. They accomplish all of this while shuffling around in their favorite pairs of flip flops in ⁻10-degree weather. Who cares about proper footwear for the elements? Where they're going, sandals will suffice for the week.

Passengers are on their way to warmer temperatures, like kids on Christmas morning, impatiently awaiting the opportunity to bury their toes in the sand, snap selfies in front of the crystal clear turquoise waters, and drink as much all-inclusive liquor as their livers can handle. But before they can dive into their piña coladas, they must legally enter the country of their destination by completing their customs declaration and/or immigration forms.

If you haven't flown internationally in a while, then it would be helpful to familiarize yourself with the requirements for entering a foreign country. Passengers have approximately three hours to complete a form assessing their understanding of brain surgery, rocket science, and possible cures for cancer—filling in both sides, front and back. Just kidding. Kind of.

You would think that the answer to world peace depended on the correct completion of these forms. If I had a dollar for every question I had to answer about customs declarations and immigration forms in my career, I could have retired two years into flying. During my time working international flights, I have learned that inevitably, any flight requiring form completion will bring out four types of passengers:

> *The Insecure One.* Do you remember that kid in school who always had to complete everything perfectly? I'm talking about the one who monopolized the teacher's time and wouldn't allow the teacher to step away because he needed assurance that each step of the process was completed without even the slightest error! That's this passenger! The Insecure One never asks to borrow a pen because he brought his own pens with the comfortable grips in an array of colors. The form will be completed correctly on the first try, so don't worry about needing extra forms for this pas-

senger—the flight attendant will be holding his hand the whole time.

The Independent One. The flight attendants' favorite. She's the person who listens to instructions, reads the forms, and simply does what is asked. She also only needs one form, because she can read and follow instructions the first time. She may ask to borrow a pen but will most likely remember to return it to the flight attendants.

The Inattentive One. While not as needy as the Insecure One, the Inattentive One rings the call light to ask for a second form because when he filled out his date of birth, he put the month and then the day instead of switching them. His error was due to missing the announcement when the flight attendants warned of this adjustment not once, not twice, but three times after distributing the forms. He's going to need a pen and will likely not return it because his nervousness led to him knocking it off his tray table and it falling under the seat in front of him.

The Indifferent One. She's likely to ask you for a form on the final approach for landing because she was sleeping during the distribution of forms and hasn't quite realized that the flight attendants have already tucked one away in her seat pocket. If she doesn't know the address of the hotel where she is staying, she'll just leave it blank. Oh, and don't worry, she doesn't need a pen. She'll just fill it out with a toddler's crayon that rolled under her seat and she found during takeoff, or the pen an Inattentive One in the seat behind her just knocked off his tray table.

A trip to Cabo San Lucas was no exception when the cast of four types of characters sprinkled themselves aboard our aircraft that would whisk them away to their paradise vacations. Following take off, the flight attendants took to the aisles to distribute the customs declarations and immigration forms to allow time for questions and concerns to be addressed during the flight.

Directly after the distribution of the forms, one of my colleagues took to the microphone and made an announcement regarding some of the common mistakes made when filling out the forms, like how to correctly fill in the dates (see "The Inattentive One" above), and how specific blocks only need to be completed if a passenger is moving to the foreign country permanently. As the announcement continued, I was passing back and forth through the cabin addressing different concerns and making runs for supplies for service. Toward the back of the aircraft, I happened to notice a row of jovial women, all traveling together, ready to commence vacation.

The women were undoubtedly related. The resemblance between them was uncanny and the way they reached across one another sharing snacks and poking to get each other's attention led me to believe that a girls' trip was probably a regular occurrence with these three. Passes up and down the aisle so far allowed me to hear components of their conversations that helped me piece together their relationships and some of the characteristics of their personalities.

Two of the women appeared to be in their late thirties, displaying a bond that only sisters have and joking sweetly throughout the flight. Joining them was their mother, a woman likely in her sixties with strong facial features that both of her daughters had inherited.

All three women were unapologetically dressed for vacation success; dress for the vacation you want to have! If their outfits were any representation of what their vacation was going to be like, then watch out, because these women were ready for a party. Each donned a T-shirt in a different shade of neon pink — *Who knew there could be so many shades of hot pink?!* — with a vacation slogan in bold white block letters, like "Ready for a beer in my hand and my feet in the sand!" The sisters had a little wild side to them, though. One sister's shirt used a darker shade of pink to create a pattern that resembled a cheetah print, while the other sister sported a similar shirt that highlighted a zebra print.

As my colleague continued to make announcements regarding the forms, I had just finished up with a textbook Insecure One and was headed to the back of the cabin to set up the carts for a drink and beverage service. Walking up and down the aisle, I try to be cognizant of what passengers around me are saying, because it's likely that they have questions. If I overhear the questions, I can address them before a mistake is made, or I can be proactive in avoiding the ringing of a call light to answer questions while I'm slinging sodas.

At this point in the announcement, the flight attendant was providing some helpful tips regarding the destination that would need to be input in a couple of the boxes. She continued, "Ladies and gentlemen, if you look closely at questions 12 and 13, you'll see that you need to fill in the city and state that you'll be visiting. For question 12, this will be the city that you are visiting, which is simply Los Cabos. Continuing with question 13, this is the state where Cabo is located: Baja California Sur, Mexico — and it's okay to abbreviate the state with the letters B.C.S."

At the exact moment that the Lead Flight Attendant said the word "Mexico," I happened to be one row behind the "Pink Safari Ladies." At the window seat was Sister #1, AKA "Cheetah," who I pinned as an Insecure One. Next to her was Mom in the middle seat, who I undoubtedly categorized as an Independent One. And, finally, in the aisle seat was Sister #2, AKA "Zebra," who had taken after her mother and exhibited signs that she was also an Independent One.

My ears perked up because I heard what seemed to be the rumblings of the start of a question in Pink Safari Ladies Row. I stopped in my tracks and turned around to try to catch the question that was being asked. Luckily, I didn't address them, but simply stood a row behind listening to the entire conversation before interacting. Cheetah, in true disbelief, stuttered, "Wait ... what did she just say?"

Zebra, offering a matter-of-fact response repeated. "She just said to write 'Los Cabos' for the city and 'B.C.S.' for the state." Cheetah quickly dismissed the answer her sister provided and inquired about a more unsettling piece of information that she was sure she misunderstood. "No! What did she say at the end? I thought I heard her say 'Mexico!'"

"You did hear her say, 'Mexico,'" Mom confirmed. Cheetah turned to her sister and mother with anger in her eyes and bellowed, "WHAT?!" Her exclamation was followed by an extremely long pause and awkward stares between the three. Breaking the silence, Cheetah tried to unveil what she thought was a prank. "The attendant was kidding, right?! We're not going to Mexico for real, are we?

Mom and Zebra stared at each other with confusion and I stood back enjoying the revelation while wondering, *How in the world did you get this far and not know that you were going to Mexico?!* Zebra then asked what my next question would have been. "Where did you think we were going?"

Cheetah tried to hold herself together but was obviously freaking out. "I didn't know that Cabo was in Mexico! Why would you choose this place?! IT'S NOT SAFE THERE!" Mom intervened by encouraging Cheetah to calm down. She assured her that it was safe and that Cabo was filled with pools, beaches, and tourists.

Then Mom looked at Cheetah for an explanation. "We made you get your passport for this trip. What country did you think we were going to?"

Cheetah was completely distraught by this point. "I thought Cabo was its own country. If I had known it was in Mexico, I would have never agreed to this."

Zebra was annoyed that her sister was causing a scene and had such a negative reaction. Attempting to calm her down, she said, "For real, you need to chill. We're going to have fun! The pictures look beautiful!"

Cheetah looked like she was about to explode, and her mind was clearly spiraling out of control. She started moving frantically in her seat, making exaggerated hand and arm gestures. Had it been physically possible to open a window, I think she would have felt safer taking her chances jumping out and using her hot pink cheetah print mess of a shirt as a make-shift parachute to land her somewhere mid-Nebraska. At least they would have been able to spot her upon landing.

Cheetah exclaimed, "I'm sure the pictures *do* look great! But I know better, I've been watching the news!" She tapped the TV monitor in front of her several times with quite some force as the scrolling words at the bottom of the screen emphasized securing the United States' borders. All the while gesturing to the TV monitor, Cheetah continued, "Mexico is full of drug cartels and crime—that's why they're building a wall, and you want me to chill out and be excited to go on this vacation?! You're both crazy!"

Mom and Zebra were beside themselves. They had both done their research and knew that their vacation destination was completely safe. I could tell as I made my way past them that they were both disappointed in the way their third was acting. Cheetah truly believed that they would all be in danger if they continued with this trip. She began to self-soothe, backing into the corner where the side of the fuselage meets the end of her seatback, while Mom and Zebra continued to meet eyes with disbelief and sit in awkward silence.

Business continued as usual and my fellow flight attendants and I took to the aisle to offer the finest selection of drinks and snacks. We continued row by row until we reached the Pink Safari Ladies. As luck would have it, I ended up being the one who served them. While I had been privy to the entire scene they'd made earlier, the three had been too wrapped up in each other to notice that they'd had spectators other than the folks in front of and behind them. I thought I might try to calm Cheetah down while also having some fun.

I asked the ladies if I could offer them beverages. While Zebra and Mom politely asked for a Diet Coke, Cheetah could only utter one brief question: "Do you have alcohol?"

Happy to share that I had what Cheetah requested, I responded, "I sure do. All our alcohol is for purchase. What did you have in mind?"

"Do you have whiskey," Cheetah asked, "and can I have two?"

Shooting her a warm smile, I asked, "Rough morning? Our margaritas are the featured drink! I can't think of anything that will get you more in the mood for your MEXICAN vacation than tequila!" She denied my suggestion and stuck with her original order of whiskey and Coke.

As I read Cheetah's expression, I could tell that the word "Mexican" increased her anxiety and her need for alcohol. I softened my approach. "You doing all right? Anything I can do to help?" Mom stepped in to speak for her, scared that Cheetah might be on the verge of a nervous breakdown. "She'll be all right, she's just nervous about going to Mexico, what with them always being in the news and building a wall and stuff."

"Oh, I gotcha. Is this your first time going to Mexico?" I asked. Mom told me that both her and Zebra had been before but that this trip would be Cheetah's first time. While I was passing off drinks, I offered my views on Mexico in the hopes that it would calm Cheetah. "Oh, okay. Well, there's no reason to be nervous. I promise you, it's safe and it's so beautiful. Our pilots and flight attendants have layovers there all the time. On every single flight home that I've ever worked from Cabo, all my passengers are miserable. And the only reason they're miserable is because they don't want to leave the amazing beaches, wonderful food, and all the unlimited liquor. Really, it's an amazing resort town. You're going to have a blast. If you really don't want to go, you can work the flight back for me and I'd be happy to sip margaritas in my bikini in your place!"

They all giggled at the thought of me rocking a bikini. The visible tension in Cheetah's body seemed to release, if only outwardly. Perhaps my experience with flying to these destinations helped to ease the stress. Hearing the description from me seemed to calm Cheetah more than hearing it from her mother or sister. As I was ready to pull away, I added, "Now, you ladies have a wonderful time! Soak up some sun for me and enjoy those beautiful beaches. Just beware of the tequila. I hear Mexico imports it from the country of Cabo San Lucas, and that's uncharted territory."

Mom and Zebra immediately laughed as they realized that I must have eavesdropped on Cheetah's realization that Cabo wasn't its own country. Cheetah continued sucking down her whiskey and Coke, while cracking a fake half-smile of disapproval in my direction.

Frequently Asked Questions

What are the most productive steps to take if my flight is delayed, and I have a connection I don't want to miss?

Delays happen sometimes no matter what airline you fly. We wish we could promise that every flight was going to leave on time every single time, but sometimes unforeseen circumstances arise due to weather or maintenance. In those cases, we need your help to make things flow smoothly and quickly. Safely step on board, find your seat, stow your items, and step out of the aisle. But for the love of all things good, please don't stop the flow of traffic to tell the welcoming flight attendant that you have a connecting flight that you're worried about missing. Pausing boarding isn't getting you there any faster nor is it giving you a better chance to make your flight. Let us help you become familiar with the airport and find your connecting gate once we're up in the air and on our way!

The Flight Flight

O n Day 1 of flight attendant training we focused on the human component of the industry and how it would tie into the job description. One of the very first things that was stressed during orientation was that when working in an industry where you are caring for people consistently, you will come across a myriad of stories. The stories will be of people who will be traveling to celebrate a friend's birthday, to transport an organ for a life-saving surgery, to interview for a dream job, or to say a final good-bye to a dear grandparent. As I considered the wide range of travelers that I would interact with when I started this new job, the idea of everyone having a story stuck with me.

A passenger brought a story with her on the plane one morning that I would never forget. A woman in her mid- to late-thirties walked onto the plane with multiple bags in tow. She carried a few different plastic grocery bags full of clothes and shoes, and a purse with her most important documents and necessities. While normally I tried to be consistent with enforcing the two-carry-on rule, I sensed that something was strange about this situation.

I saw from the way that she was moving, carrying these items was cumbersome for her. *Perhaps, she would have been grateful to have less bags to carry*, I thought. Knowing we had durable and larger bags that we used to collect garbage, I asked the woman, "Would it be helpful to try to consolidate a few of your smaller bags into one of our larger garbage bags so that you won't have to try to navigate your travels with so many little ones?" She seemed grateful for the offer.

I made a quick run to the galley to retrieve a garbage bag that I held open upon my return. She reached into her smaller bags and began to transfer items into the larger bag for easier transport. She moved slowly as she picked up each item from the grocery bags. Her movements were sloth-like, as if something seemed to be physically bothering her. I couldn't pinpoint it, though. I wasn't sure if she had just had a major surgery or maybe had broken an arm that she was carefully nursing. She just seemed to be in a very serious amount of pain. I asked her if I could do anything else to help, but she declined and shared that she just wanted to rest. I told her to make herself comfortable while we finished boarding.

The flight departed at an ungodly, early hour. Passengers had fallen asleep prior to the boarding door even being closed and I certainly wasn't surprised that the passenger who I helped with the grocery bags simply wanted to rest. Since the flight left so early, it wasn't quite as full of passengers as normal. The passenger with the multiple bags, let's call her Ms. Payne, asked if anyone would be sitting beside her because she was hoping to put her legs up for a little while. I told her that we weren't expecting the plane to be full this morning and she would most likely be able to settle into the extra seats. She thanked me and smiled back through all the pain she was trying her best to ignore.

Boarding was mostly finished as we waited for one more passenger. All the flight attendant duties were completed and one of my colleagues was walking towards me with a concerned look on her face. She pulled me into the galley and explained that another passenger overheard Ms. Payne talking on the phone in the gate area. The passenger was concerned that Ms. Payne may need some support. She just didn't feel comfortable approaching the situation on her own, so she thought it might be best if she told the flight attendants.

I explained to my colleague my brief interaction with Ms. Payne. I had offered her the larger bags to consolidate her belongings and I had noticed that she seemed to be in pain. She had been wincing and moving very slowly. My colleague assured me that she would check in on this passenger and see if there was anything that we could do to help her.

After several minutes of sitting and chatting, I saw my colleague lean in to give Ms. Payne a gentle hug. My colleague returned to share the details that she had learned from the conversation. Ms. Payne was fleeing from a situation of domestic violence. This morning, she snuck out of the house collecting as many of her belongings as she could, shoving them into the plastic grocery bags that she lugged onto the plane. I had been complaining about how tired I was from having to wake up at 3:00 A.M. and suddenly my heavy eyelids seemed trivial when I thought about what this woman must have gone through just to make it to the airport this morning.

After taking off and completing our beverage and snack service, the other flight attendant and I convened to discuss what we could do to help this woman. We were able to see that she was flying coast to coast that day; she would have a full day of flying ahead of her. We thought about how we could make her connection in the airport a bit smoother and what other obstacles she might encounter throughout her day that we could anticipate and assist her with.

We put our heads together to brainstorm a plan of how we would lighten the load for this woman and got to work on messaging our contacts on the ground to put the plan into action. Ms. Payne was making her way to the rear of the aircraft where we were meeting so that she could use the restroom. We told her that we had some information for her whenever she was finished, and upon her exit we asked if we could chat with her for a moment.

The other flight attendant started by explaining our goal. "We want to do everything we can to help make today a little easier for you. You're safe with us now. We took care of setting some things up for you, but if there's anything else that you think that you'll need, or if you're not comfortable with anything we've done, please let us know!"

I continued, "First, we put together a bag of snacks and drinks for you to take. We didn't want you to have to worry about getting food in the airport with your tight connection and we wanted you to have some options if you got hungry. If there is anything in there that you want more of, it's all yours!"

The other flight attendant stepped in with our next course of action. "We've contacted our managers because oftentimes they have spare suitcases for when a flight attendant's suitcase breaks in the middle of a multi-day trip. We told them that this was an extreme circumstance, so they're bringing us a suitcase that we'll be able to pack all your belongings in for you and you won't have to carry the big garbage bag."

I could see that Ms. Payne breathed a painful sigh of relief. We weren't stopping there. I continued explaining, "The gate agent for your next flight has been notified to check the suitcase so that you can send it on its way and pick it up at your last stop. This way, you won't have to lift it or worry about lugging it around. You just make sure you have your purse and any important documents that you'll need. Lastly, we've contacted our arrival gate to let them know that you'll need a wheelchair and escort to your next gate. Your connecting gate is not far from our arrival gate, but with the escort you'll be taken directly there, and they'll help you get situated with your bags. We can tell it's hard for you to breathe, so we thought you'd benefit from the wheelchair service and not having to carry your bags."

Then the other flight attendant chimed in, "And we'll be walking with you to make sure everything is taken care of for you along the way.

Tears began running down Ms. Payne's face. Between all of the stress required just to get her to the airport and the relief that came with the realization that she had finally broke away from the chains that were holding her in that abusive relationship, the flood gates had opened. She sobbed and we could tell that the emotions had taken over her body. We tried to console her and calm her as the hysterical crying was visibly painful to her. After a few moments of letting those emotions out and expressing her gratitude, she wiped her eyes and gained her composure. She began sharing her intimate story phrase by phrase, because uttering a few words at a time was all the pain she could tolerate.

Ms. Payne slowly spoke each word. "Last night he was so angry, and I asked him to calm down. He threw me down the stairs. I was in shock. My body hurts so badly," she said tearing up. "I think my ribs might be broken." Worried that she sustained a serious injury, I asked if she wanted us to organize paramedics to meet the flight to check her out. She graciously denied the offer knowing that she had a tight connection for the flight that would take her to her parents. "When I get there, then I'll go to a hospital," she assured us.

The other flight attendant took a moment to validate the efforts that Ms. Payne made this morning. "You did the right thing. How brave of you to make the move to leave him and get on this flight!"

Feeling safe to share, Ms. Payne opened up to us. "I knew I had to. It had never gotten that bad. For the first time, I felt like he would have killed me if I had stayed." I saw that she was reliving recent events in her head and the fear rushed back as she recalled the details.

"This morning," she started, "I snuck out of the bedroom, grabbing what I could while he was still sleeping. I was walking down the stairs and I accidentally dropped the keys. I thought for sure he would either hear the rattling of the keys or my muffled screams of pain from bending over to pick them up. I thought that one of those sounds would wake him up, for sure, and it would all be over."

We all shared the same sentiment: We were so glad he didn't wake up and so glad Ms. Payne made it here to our flight. She concurred and recapped the rest of the morning. "The Uber driver was right outside the house and he helped me get settled in quickly so we could drive away without any issues. I've been on edge all morning, wondering if he would catch up to me before I got through security and to the gate. I'm so grateful you guys have this early flight. I feel so much better now that I'm here and we're on the way."

Still concerned that she might not be out of the woods yet and that she might need some more assistance, I pried a bit further. "Please don't think that I'm trying to take away from your moment of relief, but do you have concern that he would potentially come after you? Would it be helpful if we research some contacts for you to get in touch with to be sure you remain safe after your last flight is over?"

Ms. Payne thanked me for my genuine concern but assured me that her parents were already on top of it. She was sure that as soon as she got to them all these worries would be taken care of. "Also," she added, "unless he plans on driving across the country, I don't think he'll be able to get very far if he decided to come after me with a flight. When I went into my wallet to show my ID at security, I realized that I had his driver's license in there. He makes me carry it around for him when we go out with friends because he doesn't want to bring his wallet. He doesn't have any other form of picture ID—no passport or anything. I may or may not have *accidentally* flushed his driver's license down the toilet in there."

I chuckled to myself then said, "We certainly don't encourage flushing foreign objects down the toilets of our lavatories, but what can you do? Accidents happen! You let us know if you need anything else. We're here for you."

When we arrived, we helped Ms. Payne get all of her belongings switched over to a suitcase, we checked her bag to her last stop and made sure that the next set of flight attendants knew to take care of her for the second leg of her travels. I was sad for her and that she had to go through such a terrible experience, but I was hopeful that she was going to be safe now. I was proud of her for being so strong through it all. I was proud of our team for finding ways to make one woman's journey better and help her safely get to her destination.

Ms. Payne's situation got me thinking about the baggage that passengers bring with them on the plane. I had a realization: We all have points in our lives where we feel like we're the ones lugging several grocery bags. I've certainly had moments where I wished someone would appear with a roll-aboard suitcase to lighten my load, but gratefully, I've never had to endure physical and emotional pain like the situation that Ms. Payne experienced. I knew that Ms. Payne's journey was far from over and that it wouldn't be an easy one, but I was happy to know that I could play a part in exchanging her grocery bags for a roll-aboard suitcase.

Did You Know

Each alcoholic drink consumed in the air typically has the same effect on your body as two drinks on the ground. Your blood alcohol level in the air won't be any different than it would be on the ground, but the altitude plays a part in how your body is affected by alcohol. While three drinks on the ground might not have much of an effect, three in the air might have you singing at the top of your lungs to your favorite track that's blaring through your headphones. Other passengers bought tickets to fly to their destinations of choice. They didn't buy tickets to your solo concert.

Percentage of Pettiness

"I'll have a large latte with three extra shots of espresso, two pumps of cinnamon syrup, two pumps of sugar-free vanilla syrup, five pumps of white mocha syrup, half almond milk, half skim milk with extra whipped cream, caramel drizzle on top, oh, and extra hot." Raise your hand if you've ever stood in line behind someone at the coffee shop and you heard an order like that. I'm raising my hand.

In addition to ordering a drink that requires fluency in some alternative barista language, the person is usually not polite when asking for it, *and* is the first to make a huge scene when one component of the 735 ordered is missing or crafted incorrectly. Now, I recognize I'm making a broad generalization here, but aren't we all familiar with how that scenario plays out? We see the barista recoil, "I'm so sorry, I must have only put four and a half pumps of white mocha in. I'll remake it for you because the customer is always right." Let's go with that mantra: the customer is always right!

If the customer is always right, then let's allow him to be right, I thought as I met the main character of this story. Our beverage service began, and I made my way through the cabin when I arrived at row 25. I greeted the passenger there as I would any other, "Hi, sir. How are you today?"

With no interest in niceties he arrogantly responded, "Thirty percent cranberry juice, seventy percent orange juice, and one ice cube. Can you handle that?"

Many times, before I even get the chance to say anything to the passengers, they call out their drink and snack orders. I'm not bothered by it. I think the passengers are just trying to be efficient. They know why I'm standing in front of them with a big metal cart, most of the time, so why not show some initiative and holler out their choices without making me ask? When this happens, I reorder the flow of my interactions, and I utilize the time I'm pouring their drinks to ask how they are doing and share in the light conversation that I would have if I had the opportunity to ask prior to taking drink orders. No big deal!

In this case, I thought to myself that the interaction felt abnormal. The gentleman in 25C seemed arrogant and inherently defensive — as if he might intentionally be looking for a fight? I looked at him and thought, *I serve sodas, sir, and nothing about a can of cola is worth fighting over*. I approached him politely as I approached the other hundred passengers that I served. Disregarding my niceties, he just couldn't help himself. He had to throw in that zinger at the end, "Can you handle that?" I've developed a thick skin over time and I've also learned that 99% of the negative interactions that happen on airplanes aren't personal. Ultimately, these negative interactions seem to be reflective of the frustrations that the passenger may have experienced throughout the day and have just now decided to misdirect at the flight attendants.

I had had no prior interaction with 25C, and I brought nothing but a pleasant attitude to the conversation, so I can only assume that this is more about him and less about me. I haven't kicked the back of his seat, I didn't spill anything in his lap, and I didn't kill his first-born child, so I think we're all good here. But when he chose to make a remark that assumed I had a lower level of intelligence than he and I lacked the ability to "keep up" with his lame-ass order, then school needed to be in session. So, while a soda might not be worth fighting over, a lesson on the proper way to treat a human being always is.

I smiled at 25C and obliged. I grabbed a plastic cup and I eyed it for a solid 15 seconds. I tilted my head to the side and pretended to look at the curvature of the cup in the same way that my students looked at me the day I introduced their first lesson on imaginary numbers. I'd try my best to most accurately measure out 30% of one liquid. I grabbed the can of cranberry juice, flicked open the tab, and began pouring, all the while smiling excessively at 25C. I estimated what appeared to be about 30% and then held the cup at eye level. I inspected the amount and judged that I'd only reached approximately 29%, so another splash was imperative.

As I poured the first portion of my cocktail of juices, the lovely lady in 25B observed my actions with a grimace on her face. She grinned at me with a snicker as to say, "I'm picking up what you're putting down, and I'm here for it." She had heard the entire dialogue between the two of us and she continued laughing to herself. Fortunately, her location in 25B was on the opposite side of the aisle from 25C, so my beverage cart perfectly blocked the gentleman from view of her giggles while I reveled in the fact that someone else would get to enjoy this moment with me. Instead of a solo production, why not make it a duet by giving 25B a speaking part in our little roleplay lesson?

Keeping a straight-face, I looked to the woman in 25B. "Miss, may I bother you for a moment for some assistance? In your opinion, do you think this cup is 30% full of cranberry juice? I want to get it just right."

She played along as I hoped. "Yep, that looks exactly like 30% to me."

"I don't know," I said, "I think it's just a little short of 30%. Maybe I need just a small bit more."

The woman in 25B continued to laugh at the level of pettiness I had achieved and I allowed the can of cranberry juice to tilt just in the slightest so that a drop poured out into the cup—*now* it's 30%. All the while, the gentleman in 25C looked like he might explode because his absurd order had turned into an unexpected scene at 32,000 feet in the air.

I decided that while I had enjoyed playing out the comedy, I had spent an exorbitant amount of time pouring one silly drink and the rest of the cabin shouldn't have had to suffer as a result of 25C's rudeness. I grabbed the can of orange juice, topped off the glass and gingerly plopped in the one ice cube requested. Might I say that one ice cube was going to do nothing in the grand scheme of chilling a beverage, so he should have just ordered 30% cranberry juice, 65% orange juice and 5% water. Regardless, I passed the concoction off to him exactly how he ordered it.

I looked to 25C as I asked for approval. "Well, how did I do? I've never been great at math. I hope I made it correctly." He exhaled an indecipherable grumble that showcased his disdain for me and my choice to make a fool out of his attempt at establishing superiority. Knowing that whatever he uttered would be lacking any sense of gratitude and wouldn't be worth hearing clearly anyway, I didn't bother to ask him to repeat himself. I just smiled and moved on with the conversation.

"Sir, may I get you a snack? I have cookies, peanuts, or pretzels," I offered.

"Cookies and peanuts," he answered. His order was quite the opposite of his absurdly specific drink order. I was fully expecting him to ask me to warm his peanuts in the oven prior to serving them to him. Maybe my little roleplay taught him a lesson!

Just to be sure he knew who he was dealing with, I offered one last remark as I collected his snack choices. "I do have to say, I am *so* glad that you ordered with percentages, because had you ordered with fractions, I don't think I would have ever gotten it right!" He snatched the snacks out of my hand, as expected, and I rolled right on with my beverage cart knowing he heard my unspoken "screw you" loud and clear.

TRAVEL TIP

Turbulence: you either love it or you hate it. Some passengers love turbulence so much that they wish for it to happen to rock them to sleep. Other passengers experience turbulence and they are stunned with immediate fear and anxiety. When passengers are concerned about turbulence, I try to ease their stress by explaining it as simply as possible.

Start by thinking about a raft on water. While floating, you may tighten your grip on the raft handles, or grab hold of your sunglasses in anticipation of larger waves, but you probably wouldn't be bothered by those larger waves because you could see them coming. You'd know what to expect, right? In the air, the pilots are watching for waves using cutting-edge technology and up-to-date information from Air Traffic Control. The difference between a raft and the plane is that we can't see the waves in the air so we can't prepare for them in the way we would on a raft.

Thinking of the airplane riding the waves in the sky usually helps connect air travel to an image that's somewhat relaxing. While the pilots do their best to avoid those waves, they can't guarantee that some of them won't feel like tsunamis, which is why you should always keep your seatbelt fastened any time you're not moving around the cabin. And if you're still scared, just take a peek at the flight attendants, because the turbulence you're experiencing is probably normal. So, if the flight attendants aren't losing their shit, then no need to lose yours!

Open-Door Policy

"I'm not feeling well" is one of my least favorite phrases to hear on an airplane. For some reason, when I hear that phrase I have a flashback to teaching fifth grade when one of my students threw up all over the classroom, so maybe it's a little bit of education PTSD, but the anxiety is real. Such a phrase can mean several different things. Are we talking about feeling a heart attack coming on, or is it just the turbulence causing a little bit of motion sickness? Either way, please don't throw up on me.

Boarding had almost ended for my last flight of the day. My crew and I had finished a tiring day of flying and now it was time to head home on the final flight of our trip. When normally our flights were nearly full, if not 100% full, this flight would be a little treat because we had anticipated that a quarter of the aircraft would be empty. What a breath of fresh air, especially that this was the last flight of the night—this would be a stress-free evening! Passengers had no problem finding spots for their bags, boarding seemed to flow smoothly, and the frantic requests for assistance prior to takeoff seemed to be at a minimum.

We took off and everything went off without a hitch until the dreaded "tap." Tap, tap, tap on my shoulder. I immediately thought, *Why is someone touching me? Are you a kindergartener who knows no better?* Of course, it wasn't.

I turn around and there stands Mr. Gray. This wasn't his actual surname, but a name I bestowed upon him because it appropriately matched the shade of his complexion. Mr. Gray was obviously not feeling well. He made a motion to me that requested a moment of my time in privacy to divulge some information that he felt should remain confidential.

I obliged and stepped to an open space in the last couple of rows of the aircraft, unsure of what this man was about to share with me. Mr. Gray whispered, "I was wondering if I could move to another seat. Maybe an aisle seat, if possible? Is there any chance I could sit in one of those open rows near the bathroom back there? That would be really good. It's just . . . I'm not feeling well."

That dreaded phrase—there it was. In addition to tap, tap, tapping on my shoulders and touching me with his germy hands, he had pulled me aside to share some more germs by coming in such close proximity just to whisper in my ear that he was a bit under the weather. The award for the Sickest Close Talker went to Mr. Gray. While I was no medical professional, I wanted to do my best to make Mr. Gray feel better, if there was anything within my power. Let's figure out what "not feeling well" meant.

"Okay, well let's go ahead and start by having you take a small step back," I suggested. "We don't want to spread any more germs than we need to. Can you share with me some of the symptoms you're having? Are you feeling nervous to fly? Is this the flu? What's going on?"

Mr. Gray took a couple steps back to comply with my request then continued, "Oh, I'm fine with flying. I'm not sure what it is, though. Definitely something with my stomach. I don't feel achy or flu-like symptoms. I really don't have any other symptoms so I'm beginning to wonder if it's some type of food poisoning. Maybe it was something that I ate! I've been in and out of the bathroom for the last several hours."

While I certainly hadn't wished food poisoning upon anyone, I was slightly relieved to know that the reason that Mr. Gray was feeling the way he was could be traced back to some spoiled food, rather than some contagious illness that the passengers and crew needed to be worried about contracting. But could you imagine having to take a three-hour flight with food poisoning? No thank you! The two biggest reactions to food poisoning are no secret and if you've ever had it, then you're aware of the absolute necessity of a nearby, consistently available bathroom. Having understood the state of the ill passenger, I permitted him to occupy the row he requested, which was five rows from the back. Sitting there, he would be near the aircraft's two rear lavatories.

Stepping back into my galley, I resumed my responsibilities preparing the beverage and snack carts for the service that the crew and I would offer in a few short moments. I was nearly ready to head into the aisle to begin service when Mr. Gray snuck up behind me. "Hey! Do you think I could have a glass of water?" I was happy to pour him one.

I turned around to grab a plastic cup and a bottle of water, and in the few seconds it took for me to unscrew the cap from the bottle, he stealthily disappeared into the lavatory. I assumed that based on the conversation we had had at the beginning of the flight and the state of his health, he may have had a lavatory emergency that had caused him to bail on his request for a glass of water. Realizing that Mr. Gray was no longer standing there and that he may have needed a minute before he returned to the galley to claim his water, I set it aside in the galley and completed the final touches for setting up the cart.

As I finished up, another gentleman arrived at the rear of the aircraft, hoping to find a vacant lavatory. I heard the rustling of the lavatory door behind me and then with a flutter, I heard the unsuspecting gentleman apologizing profusely for opening a restroom while Mr. Gray was occupying it. I asked the gentleman if everything was okay.

"Yeah. I'm sorry," he responded. "I opened the door on that guy while he was using the restroom. I didn't know anyone was in there—it was unlocked." I would have done the same thing if the door were unlocked.

To ease his embarrassment I apologized saying, "I'm sorry that happened. While I'm sure it's far from comfortable to walk in on another passenger amidst their time in the restroom, the situation could have been avoided if he would have locked the door, no?"

The unsuspecting gentleman agreed and laughed off the awkwardness of having seen a grown man doing his business on an aircraft. He sheepishly cowered back into the aisle as he awaited the moment when he and Mr. Gray would be forced to pass one another, and he would have to look Mr. Gray in the eye.

I attempted to intervene, gently knocking on the door of the lavatory Mr. Gray occupied to offer some advice. "Sir, please make sure you lock the door for your privacy." Then, I pointed out the second lavatory that was still available if the unsuspecting gentleman wanted to use it. I didn't need to tell him twice. He dove into the other restroom in the hopes of not ever having to make eye contact with Mr. Gray.

With the lavatory situation resolved, I unlocked the brakes on the cart to head into the aisle. I wrangled the cart attempting to align the wheels in the direction of the aisle and as I took a step back, Mr. Gray was there to catch me. I stumbled over his foot, realizing he had reappeared from his disappearing act. "Oh, excuse me! I'm sorry, I didn't see you behind me!" I said. Unbothered by the little dance I did on his foot, Mr. Gray asked if he could please have the water I had poured for him. "Sure, it's right here!" I told him.

I reached over to the counter to grab the water and turned around. Before Mr. Gray could pull a fast one on me, again, I caught him with one foot inside the restroom and I handed him the water. He guzzled down the glass and asked for another. I poured him a second cup, he thanked me, and stepped back into the washroom. Again, he chose not to lock the door. I gave a quick knock and reminded him that it would be best that he locked the door when using the lavatory. I heard a loud and quick click as the green "Vacant" indicator turned red and "Occupied" was displayed.

With all requests fulfilled in the back galley and lavatory area, I finally had the opportunity to step out into the aisle and begin the beverage service. I began serving passengers and after serving three or four rows, I had a request from a passenger to purchase a food item for sale. I knew I didn't have the item stocked on the cart that I manned in the aisle, but I had plenty in the back galley. Leaving the aisle to quickly grab the item, I noticed that the restroom was still occupied. I saw that Mr. Gray wasn't in his seat and I assumed that he continued to occupy it. I knocked on the door again, then spoke in his direction. "Hello! Sorry to bother you! I'm just making sure you're feeling okay. Can I get you anything?"

Mr. Gray told me that he was fine for the moment, then asked if he could please have more water. I told him I'd set another glass of water on the counter for whenever he was ready for it. Before I walked away, I mentioned that he should ring the yellow light next to the sink if he needed anything else while I was out in the aisle serving.

I poured the glass of water and set it on the counter, grabbed the food item I originally had set out to the back galley for, and then I resumed my position on the backside of my cart. While serving from this position, my backside was facing the rear of the aircraft where the lavatories were located. Therefore, I didn't have a direct sightline to the rear of the aircraft. At best, I could use peripheral vision as I turned left or right to hand off drinks and snacks to get a full 360-degree view.

During one interaction with a passenger, I had turned completely sideways to pass a lady the two drinks that she ordered. Out of the corner of my eye I saw the figure of a man stepping into the same restroom that Mr. Gray had been occupying for most of the flight.

I wouldn't have thought twice about seeing a male figure step into a lavatory except that I noticed two interesting, and potentially startling, things about the male figure. First, he entered the restroom after coming directly from the galley area. Occasionally, passengers will step into the galley area to see if items they may need are laying out and available: a napkin, some water, or an extra snack. Sometimes passengers feel more comfortable just grabbing things they need that are sitting out rather than bothering us; however, we prefer to serve all our passengers instead of establishing a make-yourself-at-home environment. Ultimately, it's a safer and more sanitary set-up. The second, and much more alarming noticing, was that I was almost positive that the male figure was exposing his naked backside, as he hadn't completely pulled up his pants.

That couldn't have been the case, right? Was there really a guy walking around my galley with his bare behind just hanging out? My eyes were tired. I'm sure it was just a light-colored shirt hanging lower over his backside or maybe his shirt was pulled up a little bit and the flesh color was the small of his back. By this point, I was several rows closer to the rear of the cabin after serving passengers. I walked a few steps to the back of the cabin and saw that Mr. Gray was not back in his seat yet, and the door to the lavatory was unlocked for the third time. I had decided to give up on my campaign for "No Doors Left Unlocked." If he wanted people to walk in on him, that was his problem. I looked over into the galley and I saw that the water that I had set out for Mr. Gray was gone. I hadn't noticed much movement from other passengers and Mr. Gray was the only one who had been frequenting the lavatory.

I recounted the situation in my head. I created an image of the scenario of Mr. Gray having shuffled out of the bathroom with his pants half-down to grab that cup of water. It was time to be honest with myself. I knew what butt cheeks looked like when I saw them and convincing myself that he was wearing a flesh-colored t-shirt that would hang that low beyond his waistline was just stupid. While I would have loved to give him the benefit of the doubt, the way that he was shuffling so rapidly and the height of his pants on his legs gave him away.

His entire shuffle-dance was reminiscent of a toddler who finished going potty on his own for the first time. Think: little boy who waddled out of the bathroom with his pants around his ankles, wanting to grab his mother's attention for the poo celebration and reward. He discovered he could arrive at his mother's side much quicker if he pulled up the pants to his thighs to allow for longer strides. Mr. Gray seemed to be attempting to get his reward of water and then headed back into the lavatory for round 5 or 6. I had lost track at that point.

What should I have done in that situation? We hadn't addressed these types of scenarios during our training sessions. I was still only about 95% sure that I actually saw what I thought I saw. While the chances were pretty good that my mind wasn't playing tricks on me, I didn't know what the best course of action would be. What was a respectful way to tell a person that pants were required when not behind a locked bathroom door, and why wasn't this common knowledge?! Should I have knocked on the door and said, "Hey, was that your ass hanging out a moment ago when you ran in and out of my galley for water? Let's go ahead and keep your tail covered for the duration of the flight."

Exhausted from the day and having weighed all my options, I decided that I would just let that one instance slide. None of the other passengers witnessed it and I wasn't getting the vibe that he was attempting to be an in-flight flasher. He seemed to be trying to perform the "grab 'n go" very quickly as his silhouette was a blur when I had seen him enter the lavatory. Out of sympathy for his condition, I chalked it up to a personal emergency and an absolute dire need for that water. Brushing it off, I grabbed onto my cart and distributed drinks and snacks for the remaining passengers.

Approximately 10 rows from the back of the aircraft, I attempted to serve the passengers while partially distracted by quick glances to the back of the aircraft to make sure everyone was clothed. After the third or fourth glance, I let out a sigh of relief that I wouldn't be forced to initiate an awkward conversation with a grown man about being sure his naked body was covered before making a quick run to the galley for a glass of water. Just as I had let my guard down for a moment, thinking I would finish the service without a fiasco, I looked to the back of the aircraft to see the next dilemma. I excused myself from the row of passengers I was serving and bee-lined to the back of the aircraft.

Mr. Gray was not traipsing about the back galley with his pants three-fourths of the way down his thigh this time. Nope, it was much worse. The particular lavatory that Mr. Gray was using was directly in line with the aisle of the aircraft. Therefore, if I had looked straight down the center aisle from any point in the cabin, I could have seen someone entering or exiting that lavatory. Looking down the aisle, I saw that Mr. Gray was in the bathroom, his home away from home, and he had pushed the bi-fold door open. He was sitting on the commode, with his pants down around his ankles and his right foot served as the doorstop that held the door ajar. He was leaning forward, with both elbows resting on their respective knees while he cradled the glass of water using both his hands.

With a firm voice, I commanded Mr. Gray's attention. "Sir! I need you to close and lock that door immediately.

You cannot use the restroom while leaving the door open, exposing yourself." Simultaneously surprised and scared to be called out for leaving the door open, Mr. Gray immediately began apologizing and explaining. "I'm sorry. It's so stuffy in here, and it doesn't smell great. I'm getting claustrophobic and I just needed some air. I feel really sick. I'm sorry. I wasn't trying to be weird or anything."

He closed the door and locked it. I could tell from the tone of his voice that he was embarrassed to be scolded while simultaneously disappointed that he would be back behind closed doors. I couldn't even imagine what it felt like to deal with food poisoning while onboard an aircraft in a very confined bathroom space. I'm sure he was telling the truth—I wouldn't expect that it smelled great in there.

He had been in and out of the lavatory for about an hour and a half, so it made sense that he was feeling the claustrophobia setting in. In all fairness, his shirt was covering anything on the front side of his body that could have potentially been exposed. All I could figure was that he was dehydrated and not thinking clearly or maybe he thought that because it was a late-night flight, he wouldn't draw an audience and he could get away with a little extra airflow. In any case, I never had the feeling that he left the door open for an attempted exposure high.

I responded with a less forceful tone. "Sir, I am very sorry that you're not feeling well. If there's anything I can do to help, I would be glad to, but if you are using the toilet, that door must remain completely closed. I'm sure you understand that we can't have you exposed in that fashion.

Also, it's not sanitary, either. We need to keep all passengers safe."

Mr. Gray exited the bathroom and told me that he understood my explanation. He apologized again. I could see that poor Mr. Gray was genuinely apologetic for causing such a scene, so I thought I'd offer him a helpful solution to his stomach woes. "Would you like to lay down in the last row of seats? You can have the whole row to yourself and you can get comfortable." He was grateful for the hospitality and took me up on the offer. Neither of us had faith that lying flat would be the cure to his illness, but it certainly wouldn't hurt to try.

After our short conversation, he snuggled into the last row of seats to find a comfortable position. I'm sure his body was exhausted from all the overexertion he was doing in the lavatory, so it didn't take him much time to close his eyes and doze off. Just to be sure that he hadn't carried his bad habits from the lavatory out into the cabin, I specifically checked on Mr. Gray each time I walked through the cabin to collect trash. I noticed that he had the button of his jeans undone in the same fashion that one would after polishing off a second plate full of Thanksgiving dinner. One undone button was a great improvement from the previous wearing choices I last experienced when gazing into the bathroom. Poor Mr. Gray slept heavily for the last hour of the flight.

As the flight came to an end, Mr. Gray awoke from his nap and seemed to feel much better. His symptoms eased up as he remained in his seat awake with no urgent need to return to the restroom. When I checked in with him, he told me that he was feeling a bit better and that he just had one more short flight left before he would finally be home. I wished him luck on the rest of his journey. Then, I wandered off in thought about how I would have never believed anyone if they had told me that on that day I would have had to tell a grown man that he must close the door while using the restroom.

Frequently Asked Questions

I fly all the time, why do I have to pay attention to the safety video every single time?

Many of our passengers are on airplanes consistently—you might be one of them. They've listened to and watched the safety demonstration more times than I have. So, I can understand that a frequent flyer might not be the most captive audience. Just be sure you're familiar with the usable exits, as they change from aircraft to aircraft.

Other not-so-frequent flyers, however, can tend to be nervous ones. Not only do these folks find a sense of comfort in following along with the video, but they also find comfort in knowing that their fellow travelers are prepared for an emergency. Therefore, instead of trying to continue your conversation by competing with the volume of a video or an announcement, just shut it for three minutes. As soon as it's over, you can go back to talking your seatmate's ear off.

Presenting the Birds

What do you get when you combine a middle-aged woman, several "free drink" coupons and a really long afternoon flight? A headache and a scene — that's what you get. I've dealt with my fair share of intoxicated customers on the aircraft. I can't think of many situations where those scenarios ended pleasantly, but with each case I gain more on-the-job experience for dealing with passengers who can't hold their liquor.

While serving beverages from the cart, I noticed a woman sitting on the aisle who was dressed very professionally. She was in a conservatively cut blue and white floral print dress with cap sleeves. Her outfit was accessorized with a chunky dark-blue necklace and bracelets to match. Her ensemble was thoughtfully curated; her make-up and hair beautifully complemented the look. As she hunkered down with her laptop, I pegged her for a traveler who was either going to or coming from an important conference where she would be leading, or had led, a presentation for a large group of people. She was poised and well-spoken, assertive, yet polite. She was the epitome of a respected professional.

As I approached Ms. Professional, I could tell that she was deeply invested in her work, fiercely typing a reply to an e-mail. I broke her concentration to ask if I could pour her a beverage. "Yes, please. I'd love a glass of red wine, thank you! Oh, and I have a few coupons for a free alcoholic beverage." Happy to fulfill her well-mannered request, I grabbed her a split of red wine and a plastic cup, placing them down on the space of the tray table that her laptop wasn't occupying. She thanked me and before I left, she asked a favor of me. "Sir, I'm not sure if you'll be coming back through with more beverages, but would it be okay if I use an additional coupon for a second glass of wine? I'll most likely want another one. I'd be happy to get it from you now that way I won't bother you later, if that works for you also?"

Passengers make this request all the time — it's extremely common. "Can I just have two now, so I don't have to bother you later?" Absolutely. The rule is to limit alcohol to two drinks at one time to be sure that passengers aren't overserved, avoiding potential intoxication. In this case, Ms. Professional was still within the "two drink" limit, so I told her I didn't mind giving her the second bottle if she preferred to have it now. I also assured her that she was no bother and we'd be available throughout the flight whenever she was ready for the next glass if she preferred to wait. She had no problem tucking away the second split into the seat pocket and passing me an additional free drink coupon to cover her tab, so she happily accepted a second bottle. The transaction was complete, and my colleagues and I moved on with the beverage service.

Later in the flight, I walked through the aisle to collect trash. As I reached the back of the aircraft, I crossed paths with Ms. Professional. She was leaving the galley in the rear of the aircraft with a bottle of red wine. We maneuvered around each other in the middle of the aisle while exchanging smiles. I took note that she was more than likely carrying her third split of wine. Arriving in the back galley, I asked my colleague if the lady in the blue dress had purchased another red wine. She confirmed that Ms. Professional did purchase a third bottle with a coupon and then my colleague asked me if I had served her during the beverage service. I explained that I gave her two splits of wine during the service so the split that was most recently purchased would be her third. My colleague assured me that she wasn't exhibiting any signs that would lead her to believe that Ms. Professional was intoxicated.

All seemed to be fine until my other colleague was walking through the aisle passing out glasses of water and Ms. Professional caught her attention. With a fourth coupon in hand she said, "May I have a glass of red wine, please. Here's a coupon." The third colleague passing out waters was out of the loop regarding my earlier discussion with the other flight attendant. She was unaware that this woman had already consumed three splits of wine. Her interaction with Ms. Professional was also very brief. Ms. Professional requested the wine with a few polite words and had the coupon ready to pass off to her. My colleague already had Ms. Professional's form of payment and didn't need to stick around to complete the transaction on her device, so she simply dropped off the wine and continued her duties.

Because of the ease of the exchange and with essentially no tip-offs of intoxication from Ms. Professional, my colleague served her the fourth split of wine. She still exhibited no obvious signs of intoxication and the first three miniature bottles hadn't quite set in yet for anyone to feel justified in cutting her off.

After passing out water and returning from handing off the wine, the flight attendant pulled out the coupon and began setting up her device to scan the information for the completion of the sale. The flight attendant who sold the third glass of wine asked where the coupon came from. We learned that the coupon was from Ms. Professional and all three of us then realized that Ms. Professional had consumed four splits of wine in total, equating to a full regular-sized bottle of wine.

Every passenger handles alcohol differently and to some drinking a whole bottle of wine wouldn't lead to any outrageous consequences. Obviously in the interactions with Ms. Professional, none of us noticed any behaviors that signaled that she may have had enough, in which case we continued serving her. Her behavior seemed fine, until now.

Looking into the cabin, we could see that the contents of her purse had spilled into the middle of the aisle. Instead of getting up from her seat and collecting her items, she was bent over the aisle armrest reaching for a tube of lipstick, her wallet and some other small items that were housed safely in her handbag prior to the spill.

Seeing her struggle, I went out into the aisle to assist her with gathering her belongings. She continued speaking loudly to her seatmate while we collected the items together. I was much more productive with cleaning up the mess because I had a larger span of movement while kneeling on the floor instead of hanging over an armrest. She thanked me for my help as she poured the second half of the wine split into her glass. Her volume had increased to the point that other passengers were taking notice and she began slurring her words; the two signs of an obvious lack of control over her own dexterity.

I decided at that moment that we wouldn't be serving Ms. Professional any more alcohol on this flight. She had consumed four splits of wine over the course of an hour and forty-five minutes and based on my observations, she seemed to be intoxicated. I spoke with the other flight attendants and explained that she would be cut off from alcohol because she was exhibiting signs of intoxication and because she seemed to be attracting negative attention from the other passengers around her. Agreeing that we would all withhold alcohol from her, we set out into the aisle to complete a second beverage service prior to landing.

Looking through the cabin and counting the rows ahead, I calculated that I would be the one serving Ms. Professional. I was less than thrilled to have drawn the short straw because I would have to tell her that we decided not to serve her any more wine. I quickly glanced at her and I realized that the woman who had been so well put together at the beginning of the flight seemed to have transformed into a drunken mess. A sip of her most recent glass of red wine had dribbled down the front of her dress and her stained teeth, tongue and lips gave away her preference for red wine. Her heels were kicked off into the aisle, blocking the path for the beverage cart, her makeup was smudged, and her purse was spilled in the aisle again, waiting to become handbag roadkill with one of the next passes of the beverage cart.

Taking a deep breath, I reminded myself to address Ms. Professional the way I would want to be addressed if our roles were reversed. I began by speaking to Ms. Professional's seatmates first. They both denied any more beverages or snacks. Ms. Professional, however, would have a different, yet expected, response: "I'll take another red wine."

I calmly, yet firmly, stated, "I won't be able to serve any more alcohol here today, miss. Would you like a soft drink? A soda? A Juice? Some coffee?"

Ms. Professional was having a hard time processing the multiple options that I offered as substitutions. The best response she could come up with focused on just one drink. "I don't like . . . juice," she slurred. Then, I asked her if she would like something else instead.

"How much time do we have left?" she asked. I used the short remainder of flight time to attempt to deter Ms.

Professional from continuing to negotiate for more alcohol. After looking at my watch, I shared, "Well, we have about 45 minutes left, so any minute now we should be receiving the notification for our initial descent from the pilots. We're just about there."

In her book, 45 minutes was plenty of time for another drink. She changed her approach and attempted to persuade me. "Ya know, I'd be . . . really be . . . a lot more . . . much more . . . well behaved if I had one last glass of wine to sip for landing," she reasoned with her eyelids half shut. There was no chance in hell this lady was getting more alcohol from me.

"Yeah, that's not going to happen today, sorry. If you change your mind and want a soft drink, I'd be happy to get that for you."

Ms. Professional didn't care for being cut off. She was so displeased with my choice not to serve her that she decided she would put on one more presentation for the aircraft today. Her presentation of her best attempt at rebellion would be in the form of a lewd gesture for all around to see. Taking both hands, without even attempting to make eye contact with me, she flipped up the middle finger of each hand and waved them at the level of my face to be sure I clearly saw and understood her full disapproval for not being served more wine.

I knew from past experiences of drinking with friends that trying to reason through the situation was out of the question, and the best thing to do to keep a safe and calm environment for everyone was to not add fuel to the fire.

Calling more attention to her state of incoherence and continuing to decline service would likely cause more of a scene. I simply replied, "Okay then," and continued offering drinks and snacks to the passengers on the opposite side of the aircraft.

An intoxicated passenger flipping the double bird is far from threatening. I wasn't concerned for my safety, nor was I worried that Ms. Professional would lash out on one of the other passengers. The catty bitch inside of me wanted to twist open the top of a bottle of red wine and pour it on her head, but instead I kept my cool and earned accolades from the ladies sitting across the aisle from Ms. Professional. They complimented my ability to handle her rudeness. What they didn't know was that I had a double middle finger flick of my own up my sleeve; she'd find out about it later.

With the second beverage service complete and only a few minutes left before we would begin the initial descent, I decided to be productive with my downtime and do some research. As flight attendants, we are provided with a list of passengers and their connecting flights. This allows us to help passengers find their gates and other basic information regarding their connecting flights. I looked up Ms. Professional's record. I found out that her itinerary called for a connection approximately 45 minutes after we would land. One of my job responsibilities is to recognize when a passenger may be intoxicated, as the FAA enforces a regulation that airlines must deny boarding to anyone who is suspected to be intoxicated.

Unfortunately for Ms. Professional, I needed to do my job and I was sure she wasn't going to like the result. While in flight, we have a system that allows us to send messages regarding passenger needs and concerns. I took advantage of that system, opening the chat box to write the following:

Good evening,

I currently have Ms. Professional on board. She chose to consume an excessive amount of alcohol and is now exhibiting signs of intoxication. She has consumed four glasses of wine, is slurring her words, has no awareness of her volume, and is spilling on herself. She continued to request alcohol and when I denied her access to more, she decided to flip both of her middle fingers up at me and wave them around for all passengers to see. I believe that Ms. Professional will not be fit to fly in time for her next flight. Please make both the gate agents and flight attendants aware that Ms. Professional should be denied boarding as per the Federal Aviation Regulation regarding intoxicated passengers. Thank you and have a great night!

The plane landed and I returned to the messaging app to check for a response. It read:

Thank you so much for making us aware of this situation and keeping all passengers safe and comfortable! We have notified the gate agent as well as our crisis

team that will provide the proper support for this sce-
nario. Ms. Professional's record has been flagged with
a note and she will not be permitted to board the air-
craft for her connecting flight. Reservations will be no-
tified to rebook her on the next available flight to her
destination tomorrow morning at 8:00 AM.

Part of me almost felt bad, as if I were doing something malicious. While it felt like I now had my chance to give her
the finger back, realistically, part of my job is to assess all
passengers and be sure that they are fit to fly. Had I not
said something, her next crew would have been responsible
for deciding if she was fit to fly. And had she snuck onto
the plane, intoxication unnoticed, what kind of experience
was I setting our future passengers and my fellow crew
members up for?

The flight was over, the passengers had deplaned, and
the other flight attendants and I started collecting all our
belongings to deplane, as well. As we were gathering our
things, the Lead Flight Attendant inquired more about Ms.
Professional with heightened curiosity. She had only heard
bits and pieces of the most recent interactions where alcohol
was denied, but the Lead Flight Attendant seemed to have
her own story that she was dying to share with us.

"What was up with that lady? She just wanted more to
drink?" asked the Lead Flight Attendant.

"Pretty much!" I explained, "She wasn't happy that I
wouldn't give her more wine, so she decided to flip me off
with both hands in front of the other passengers."

Excited to contribute, the Lead Flight Attendant jumped in. "When she was getting off the plane, she stepped to the side and showed me a coupon that she had. She said she couldn't get wine while she was on the plane, so she wanted to cash it in for a bottle to take for the road. I told her that we weren't permitted to provide passengers with alcohol that was intended to be taken off the plane. She was pissed that I wouldn't give her the wine, so she told me I could have the stupid coupon and flicked it at me, then walked off the plane. She was such a bitch!"

I decided it was time to reveal my own surprise. "Well, don't worry. She's in for a rude awakening. What she doesn't know is that I sent a message letting the crew on her next flight know that she isn't fit to fly, and they should deny her boarding. She'll be on the next flight out tomorrow morning according to the response I got from the operation team."

The Lead Flight Attendant praised my choice to notify her next crew and confirmed that it was the right one. Having heard the Lead Flight Attendant's story, I also felt more confident and justified in making the decision to send the message that I did. The only regret I had was that I chose to go directly home instead of heading over to Ms. Professional's connecting gate. I should have stayed to watch the scene she would make as she realized she wouldn't be allowed to board the plane for her last flight.

Travel Tip

Cabin temperatures can vary greatly when flying. The summer months, especially, can require some powerful air conditioning to keep the cabin cool. I recommend dressing in layers or bringing a sweater/jacket with you to be sure you don't get too cold. The cabins tend to run cooler and, honestly, I'm glad that they do. Summertime storms create a lot of expected, and unexpected, turbulence and a cooler cabin helps to minimize the number of passengers puking and sympathy puking on the flight. There aren't enough pretzels or cans of ginger ale in all the industry that would calm motion sickness once the smell of vomit spread through a hot cabin. Yeah, even thinking about it makes me sick, too.

Stiff Drinks

The time was five o'clock in the morning. Let's just let that set in for a moment: Five. O'clock. In. The. Morning! The flight was the earliest existing flight on the airline schedule each day, excluding the ungodly hours of the night that the redeyes were departing. If the flight departed at 5:00 A.M., I can't imagine what time all the passengers had to wake up to be at the gate for boarding. While I can't think of anyone who enjoys the sound of the alarm at three in the morning, or earlier, I can understand why every flight attendant is happy to work the flight once they are awake.

Most of the passengers choose to sleep and the flight is a breeze to work. But there's always that handful of "morning people" who couldn't even consider napping on the airplane—like toddlers, once they're awake, they're awake. These adults can bounce out of bed and start their day with ease, whether this means working on a business proposal or kicking off the day-drinking.

We reached a cruising altitude and the other flight attendants, like me, slowly began to stir, wishing we had taped our eyelids open to be sure that we didn't fall asleep on the jumpseat during takeoff. Coffee pots began brewing, carts were set up for service, and most of the passengers were sawing logs, head-bobbing, drooling, or a combination of the three. We pushed the carts up the aisle to the front of the cabin to start our service. We were careful to dodge shoulders and feet, avoid aisle head-bobbers, and gracefully swerve out of the way of the limbs of children that were dangling into the aisle.

Reaching the front of the cabin we quietly asked passengers if they'd care for a beverage and the few that were awake gave a half smile and waved to signal that they'd rather continue to doze off than order a refreshment. We rolled along whispering, "No problem! Let us know if you change your mind!" Service was a breeze as we continued through the cabin — we would be done offering drinks and snacks in no time.

We pulled up to the next set of seats and secured the brake on the cart. I looked to my right and offered a, "Good morning!" to the middle-aged couple sitting next to my cart. My greeting was returned with, "Good mornin'!" in unison, in a Southern drawl. Our flight was heading south, and I assumed based on the accent that these passengers were heading home, so I asked them if my guess was correct. Taking a second to choose their words wisely, the wife responded, "Yes and no!" She explained that they were making a connection in the city that they call home, only to continue to their Caribbean vacation in the Dominican Republic.

Calmly and quietly I commented, "Well, that sounds wonderful! I bet you're excited. May I get you folks a drink this morning?"

The couple turned to each other with that questionable look of, "Is it too early to start drinking?" The wife shrugged her shoulders as if to say, "We're on vacation, so why not?" Speaking up for the two of them, she said, "We'll have two margaritas. We'll start vacation out right!"

Who am I to judge if you wanted to sip margaritas at the crack of dawn? I, personally, would have gone for the mimosa or alcoholic coffee drink route, but you like what you like! I set out two plastic cups and grabbed the ice scooper. I added one hefty scoop of ice to each glass, returned the ice scooper to the ice drawer, and bent down to open the liquor drawer that housed the miniature bottles of tequila and the single-serve margarita mixes. I snatched two of each and set them next to the plastic glasses full of ice.

Any time a passenger purchases a mixed alcoholic drink, I twist off the top of the miniature bottle, offer the bottle to the passenger, and allow the passenger to temper the strength of the drink. Following protocol, I prepared the bottles of tequila by twisting off the caps and setting them back down next to the cups. Then, I opened one of the bottles of margarita mix and just as I was about to pour it into the glass, I was startled by a booming voice, "Really? You're going to pour that in there with all that water?"

For a moment, I was rattled by the husband's unwarranted blaring volume and angered tone. I had no idea what the husband was talking about, so I apologized because I wasn't sure what he was referring to. Clearing up my confusion, he pointed to the bottom of the cup, where approximately an eighth of an inch of water pooled below the ice cubes. The ice scooper had draining slots built into it so that any of the water from the melted ice would drain back into the ice drawer and only the cubes would remain in the scoop. The minimal amount of water that collected in the bottom of the glass was a result of the ice melting. The ice sweats sitting in the bin, and even after the draining is complete the ice still melts into the glass.

I was still so confused. My mind started scrolling through some of the possible justifications for a trivial complaint about the water in his glass. First, did he think I was going to stiff him on tequila? I've watched a bartender make a drink that seemed to be light on the liquor and heavy on the mixers, so I guess this qualified as a legitimate concern. Maybe he didn't realize that I was going to hand him the entire miniature bottle of tequila. But even if the whole shot didn't fit in the glass, he could lick the bottle clean for all I cared. The amount of mixer, water or ice in the cup wasn't going to affect the total amount of tequila that he received for the price he paid. This wasn't a case where he was able to successfully negotiate to get more bang for his buck.

Secondly, was he disgusted by the idea of some of the water from the melted ice ending up in his cup? Maybe he thought the ice bin wasn't clean and he was worried about what might be floating in the water that had now been poured into his cup. That couldn't possibly be it, because obviously the ice was sitting in that water, as well. By this point, I was really just reaching to find some justification of why he might have been so offended by the water in his cup, because I was at a loss. Fortunately, I didn't have to wait very long to find out the reasoning for his scolding.

The husband told me that he didn't want water in the cup because it was going to water down the taste of the drink. He continued by telling me that if I couldn't get some of the water out of the cup, the whole drink was just going to be gross.

Annoyed at how ridiculous this whole interaction was, I flipped his cup upside down over the ice drawer and added a little extra flick of the wrist so that the ice slammed back into the drawer just to let him know my views on the absurdity of this charade. I scooped up another portion of ice, which I drained extensively to be sure I was not adding any extra water to his cup. *Boy, would I hate for his margarita to be watered down*, I thought.

He seemed satisfied that he was finally getting what he ordered. I added in the margarita mix, tossed in a stir stick, passed it off, and then handed him the bottle of tequila. I repeated these steps for his wife's drink and decided that I would also strain her ice to avoid a second round of talking-tos from the man with the finest palette for tequila and pre-made margarita mix.

The couple poured their tequila atop of the margarita mix and stirred their cocktails. While they began enjoying their drinks, I prepared a glass of orange juice for the woman who occupied the seat at the window next to the vacationing couple. As I passed her the orange juice, she smiled at me and thanked me for pouring her beverage. As I began asking what snacks I could get for each passenger in the row, the husband interrupted loudly, "See! Yeah, that's what I'm talking about. This is a good margarita. It's strong."

No offense to the airline margarita, but I can instantly think of about ten places I'd rather drink freshly made margaritas instead of the airplanes' simple syrup lime juice served from a miniature plastic bottle. The husband continued raving about the drink with his booming voice. He was speaking so loudly that passengers started to wake up.

"Babe! Babe! Did you try it? Shit's good!" he confirmed.

"Yeah, hon, it's very sweet—too sweet, I think," his wife weighed in. The husband did admit that he also thought the drink was a bit sweeter than he liked. An idea ran through my head. *You know what would have made it a little less sweet? A little bit of water in the bottom of the cup.*

I kept my comments to myself as I just wanted to get away from this row. I waited patiently to continue with snack offerings, but I couldn't get a word in edgewise. First, the husband had to offer some more feedback regarding his drink preferences. "But I like to taste the tequila, you know? I like to know there's alcohol in my drink."

His wife chimed in with her opinion as well. "Not me. I like a little bit at a time. This is too strong for me — I really could have made two drinks out of this one shot of tequila."

The two got louder as they argued over how the perfect margarita should taste and the husband stood his ground. "No, babe! It's not too strong at all. You're being a baby. I'd actually like a little more tequila in mine if I'm being honest. A double shot would really make this a drink fit for a man."

Not able to tolerate any more of the husband's inconsiderate screaming, the woman in the window seat spoke up looking him right in the eyes. "A double shot of tequila at 5 A.M. doesn't make you more manly, it makes you an alcoholic — an obnoxious one to boot."

Woman at the Window put her headphones back on, closed her eyes and leaned back in her seat to signal that she had officially had enough of the husband's loud voice and machismo mansplaining that morning. My sentiments exactly. Finally, with the couple shocked and speechless from the harsh reality that came from the woman at the window, I was given an opportunity to speak. "So, snacks anyone?" The couple declined while quietly sipping their drinks, and I happily moved on to the next row of passengers.

Did You Know

Most major US airlines allow you to select your meal option in first class prior to the day of your flight to be sure that you receive your first choice. Airlines will either provide an e-mail or an extra step during the check-in process where you can decide if you'd rather have beef or chicken, or you can select a meal for a special dietary need (e.g. vegetarian, gluten-free, etc.). While I can totally understand wanting to voice your frustration for not receiving your first choice of meal options, whose fault is it really, Mr. Smith?

Gluten-Free, Dairy-Free, Manner-Free

The day was September 11, 2016, and no matter how many years passed by, everyone was still slightly on edge, even if they didn't want to show that they were. Passengers seemed to be a little kinder and more appreciative on this day. September 11, 2001, will always be a day of terror for many who lost loved ones and will always be a day where airline workers will inevitably be on high alert. That day changed so much for so many people—and that includes every single person involved in any facet of the airline community.

I was joined by three other flight attendants, all on the younger side and most of us were relatively new to the career. I was working in the back with another young lady, while the gentleman working as the Lead Flight Attendant shared the first-class responsibilities with the young lady working in the "Helper" position up front. Even though we were all still somewhat new to the career, we were all sufficiently qualified to do our jobs. But, none of us had imagined the test of patience that we would experience with some very special passengers on today's flight.

The main cabin wasn't quite full on this particular day, and the first-class cabin was one of the larger ones in our fleet. First class was filled to the max. Additionally, the woman in the Helper position hadn't had much experience with serving in first class or with the responsibilities associated with meal distribution. We agreed as a team that we would allow her to remain in the first-class cabin with the Lead Flight Attendant so that she could shadow him and assist with his entire service in the hopes that she would become more familiar with all of the responsibilities.

While the Lead Flight Attendant and Helper kept busy in the front of the aircraft, our fourth colleague and I worked through the economy cabin with our beverage and snack service. Serving economy didn't take very long at all. With our portion of the aircraft under control and service complete, I headed up to the first class cabin to check on my other two colleagues to see if their service was going as seamlessly as ours had in the back of the aircraft.

They were moving at a slower pace than normal, but not excessively slow, so that they could serve their passengers while still allowing Helper to learn as much as she could about the process. They delivered the meals to the passengers and I could see that they had reached row 2 of 5, still three more rows to serve. I asked my colleagues if I could help in any way and they assured me that they would be done in no time, as they just had to deliver the meal trays.

Simultaneously, Helper and I stepped out into the aisle. I grabbed a trash bag to collect items as I went back through the cabin and she carried out two trays of food for passengers in row 3. As she got closer to the end of the first-class cabin, I could tell that the folks who were sitting in Seats 5C and 5D were eyeing up the options that were being served a couple rows ahead of them.

The gentleman in 5D rang his call light and caught the attention of my colleague as she was in the aisle. She headed over and I waited back a moment to listen to the request. I stayed close by in case she needed backup with an answer to a question. I learned that a husband and wife couple were sitting in 5C and 5D. The gentleman explained to Helper that his wife had changed her mind and would like to have the breakfast sandwich. He finished his request by saying, "Bring her one of those instead."

Helper was unsure if any sandwiches remained. "I'll have the Lead Flight Attendant check in with you in a moment," she told the couple. "He has the final count of all the meals, so I just want to make sure he has enough before I promise that to you."

The gentleman seemed to completely disregard anything Helper said. He responded, "Okay, but tell the lead guy she'd like to have that sandwich."

Helper smiled and nodded at the couple probably wondering if the husband understood English. That was my wondering, at least. Then, she returned to the galley to share the request with the Lead Flight Attendant. Seemingly puzzled, the Lead Flight Attendant recounted the order to Helper so they could both get on the same page regarding the interaction he had had with the couple at the very beginning of the service"

"When I approached the couple, I told them that I wanted to touch base with them regarding our offerings for this morning's breakfast. I told the lady in 5C that I could see that she selected a gluten-free meal option, and she told me that was correct. Then, she went on to explain that she also has a sensitivity to dairy products, so she wanted to know what her gluten-free meal would be. I told her that the tray had a gluten-free cereal, a gluten-free muffin with butter and jam, and a side of fresh fruit and yogurt. She had me repeat all the items, one by one, so she could veto any items that contained her specific allergens. But she didn't want me to remove any of the items that she couldn't have just in case her husband wanted them for seconds. I told her it was no problem and then I asked her husband if he cared to have the breakfast sandwich. I told him it was turkey bacon, cheddar cheese and egg on a croissant bun served with fresh fruit and yogurt. He thought it sounded great. But you're saying that now the wife also wants a sandwich?"

Helper processed everything the Lead Flight Attendant shared and then verified that 5C did, indeed, want the breakfast sandwich option. He explained to Helper that because the wife had ordered a special meal option that was tailored to her dietary needs, he wasn't able to provide her with one of the sandwiches that the husband most recently requested.

"We just don't have enough meals to serve, unfortunately," the Lead Flight Attendant said. "The catering team always provides the exact number of meals required for each first-class passenger to receive one meal." In this case, all seats were full and there wouldn't be any leftover meals. The Lead Flight Attendant assured Helper that he would go out and explain the situation to them.

"Hi, Mrs. 5C!" he began warmly, "I do apologize, but because you've listed a gluten sensitivity, catering makes sure to supply us with the gluten-free meal that accommodates your special request. Unfortunately, we don't have any extras of the two meals that the rest of first class is offered. We're given the exact number of meals for each passenger to receive one, so I don't have any extra to offer you. If I did, I would have been happy to bring you the sandwich. I'm very sorry."

Even after she was given a reasonable explanation, Mrs. 5C exploded. "I need that sandwich. I need some protein. When I take my medicine, I must eat something substantial. A little bit of dry cereal isn't going to be enough."

Hearing that medicine was part of the concern, the Lead Flight Attendant attempted to find other suitable substitutions. "I understand. Maybe I could bring you a gluten-free granola bar and a couple bags of nuts that could supplement the meal they've provided. The dairy allergy wasn't listed on your reservation, so I think that's why catering provided you the cereal with milk and yogurt, as well. I'm very sorry about that."

Realizing this interaction wasn't resolving itself, the Lead Flight Attendant headed back to the galley where he would pick up the trays of food for the husband and wife.

By this point, Helper finished serving the rest of first class while the Lead Flight Attendant was having his chat with the customers in row 5. She began collecting trays from the passengers in the first rows who had already finished eating.

The Lead Flight Attendant grabbed the trays for 5C and 5D and went into the aisle to deliver their breakfasts. He set down the trays, the egg sandwich for the husband and the gluten-free meal option for the wife. After setting down their meal options, he headed back to the galley to tidy up the area from the meal service.

As the Lead Flight Attendant and Helper were cleaning up the galley they looked up and the husband had appeared at the head of their galley, seeming very angry. He demanded, "You're going to get my wife a sandwich immediately. The meal she was given was a disgrace and there's no way that would satisfy anyone."

Still attempting to calmly resolve the situation, the Lead Flight Attendant apologized, "Sir, I am very sorry, but as I explained to you already, we do not have any more sandwiches on this plane. We have exactly enough meals for the—"

Before the Lead Flight Attendant could finish his sentence, Mr. 5D interrupted him as he moved closer. "I don't care what you have, you're going to crack some eggs and cook them for my wife, and you will make her the sandwich that she wants. She needs something substantial to eat."

Mr. 5D's approach of advocating for his wife shifted to a threat with the tone of his demands and his uncomfortable proximity to my colleagues. "Please take a step back," the Lead Flight Attendant instructed. "We don't cook food to order. Catering brings it on the plane ready to serve and we warm it up in the oven." The Lead Flight Attendant opened the carts attempting to prove to the husband that all the meals came in the cart on the trays. He wanted to show that it wasn't that he didn't want to get her a sandwich, he just didn't have any food left to give her. He wasn't catered with fresh ingredients used to cook recipes. We never are!

Still, the husband in 5D wasn't satisfied. "You can show me whatever you want. I don't care! You figure it out or else!"

The Lead Flight Attendant reached his breaking point. Sternly and with force, he ordered Mr. 5D to sit down immediately and step out of his galley. He told 5D that if he didn't get out of his face, they were going to have a big problem!

By this point, both the husband and the Lead Flight Attendant were standing in the aisle where everyone could see them. With the husband continuing to raise his voice, the Lead Flight Attendant naturally became defensive. Everyone in first class was now on high alert. I happened to be walking through the cabin toward first class and I also was able to hear the yelling between the two.

The Lead Flight Attendant was getting upset and rightfully so. He was doing everything he could to resolve the situation and was treating the husband with plenty of respect even though none was being reciprocated. He needed to put his foot down. The husband wanted him to work galley miracles. When he didn't have the supplies, there wasn't

much he could do to resolve the situation, and now this passenger was yelling in his face and bucking at him. In my
opinion, that was a terrible decision, considering that the
Lead Flight Attendant was twice 5D's size. That would be
a fight any of us would have been sure to lose. Luckily, it
never went that far.

As the husband was returning to his seat, the gentleman
in 4D turned around to address the couple with a possible
solution. "Hey, folks. I'm really not that hungry today.
Would you like to have my sandwich? I took a bite out of
it already, but it was just one bite. You can have the rest of
it if you don't mind that I already ate some of it."

The wife responded that she would love to have it. She
thought it would be lovely! She then thanked the gentleman in 4D for the offer. Her husband also thanked the gentleman and made a public statement. "See! There's always
a way to figure it out."

The gentleman in 4D assured the couple it was no problem at all. "I hope you enjoy it," he added. "You obviously
want it more than anyone else on this plane."

Are the same questions racing through your head that
were racing through mine? *Did this crazy bitch just take a
sandwich from another passenger after the passenger already took
a bite out of it?* I saw it with my own eyes. If I hadn't, I don't
know that I would have believed it. This couple who was
so delusional that they thought flight attendants were
cracking eggs and frying them up made-to-order on the airplane, were also the same people who were 100% willing
to accept a partially consumed sandwich from a complete

stranger who had already begun consuming said sandwich. Because, ultimately it made them feel important and like they had won the battle. Maybe they had won the battle, but not the war.

Watching all these events take place, I had an overwhelming amount of empathy for my poor colleagues who had been working in first class. I told my fellow flight attendants to switch with me. I offered to take care of first class, clean up trays, and deal with the delightful passengers while they went to the back and took a few moments to cool down and regroup.

Obviously, the lovely couple wasn't going to back down from any fight, and the most important goal of the trip was that we got all our passengers to their destinations safely. If that meant swallowing our pride and keeping our comments to ourselves, then we would just keep smiling and continuing to serve those disgustingly entitled human beings, because it was what we had to do to meet with success.

I went out into the aisle as a fresh face. I thought that if we did a change-up of the flight attendant cast this might make everyone feel better and alleviate some of the stress and tension between the Lead Flight Attendant and the couple. I collected trays, empty glasses, and all the other items the passengers wanted to discard while I smiled and asked if there was anything else that I could get for them. Then, I arrived at row 5. I knew that I'd have to walk on breakfast sandwich eggshells.

I noticed that the wife had a small, white, fluffy dog sitting in her lap that was registered as her emotional support animal. Perfect! I used to have a dog that looked just like this dog. This would be a great way to win them over and hopefully calm them down so that we could all get through the flight. "Hello, Mr. and Mrs. 5D! And Oh! My! Goodness! Who is this little one?" I asked.

The wife, thrilled at the extra attention, introduced me to Miss Kiki! I tried to butter up 5C by telling her that Miss Kiki was the cutest puppy I had ever seen. Then, I asked about Miss Kiki's breed. The husband confirmed that they loved their sweet pup very dearly and told me that Miss Kiki was a Maltese. I explained that I suspected she was a Maltese because I used to have one myself. I asked the couple to give me just a moment so I could run to grab a picture of my dog that I wanted to share with them.

While we were chatting, I noticed that the wife was cutting her sandwich up and alternated between eating a bite for herself and then feeding a bite to Miss Kiki! *Whatever, not my circus, not my monkeys,* I thought. *As long as she continues to be pleasant, I don't care what she does.* I went back to the galley to get my phone out to pull up a picture of my dog. Showing them the similarities between my pet and Miss Kiki, I hoped that we would share comradery and maybe, just maybe, their behavior would improve for the rest of the flight, at least with me. I returned right back with the picture.

I showed the photo and said, "This is my little guy. I think he looks so similar to Miss Kiki! What do you think?"

"Wow! They do look so much alike," the couple agreed. The wife continued praising my puppy in the picture. "He's so sweet, too! We just build such strong bonds with these dogs. They become part of our family."

"Oh, for sure!" I agreed. "You couldn't be more right!"

Feeling that we had bonded over our pets, Ms. 5C opened up more about the relationship she had with her dog. "You know, I bring Miss Kiki everywhere with me. She's my emotional support animal. She really does help me through so many rough situations. She can sense when I'm feeling anxious, and she cuddles up with me then starts howling. We howl together to get through the anxiety."

Okay, ma'am, you've lost me, now, I thought to myself. I had to draw the line somewhere. While I fully support the therapeutic abilities that animals provide for humans, I have definitely never joined my dog in unison howling. I have the ability to use my words, so I don't need to howl with him. Not letting on to how bizarre I thought this all was, I continued conversing. "I'm so glad Miss Kiki gives you comfort. I'm sure you comfort her, too, in the way you take care of her and give her such a good life!" The couple agreed.

After asking if I could get them anything else, they collectively thanked me and declined. The wife continued to alternate bird bites with Miss Kiki and the husband seemed satisfied in the moment. The Lead Flight Attendant returned to the front galley to check and see if everything was going okay. I told him not to worry and that I had everything under control. I found a way to bond with them and they were being kind to me, so I had no problem continuing to take care of the first-class cabin if he wanted to head to the back and take over my role for the rest of the flight. We just had to accept that there was no productivity in poking the bear, even if the bear deserved it.

All seemed to be right in the first-class world. All the passengers had been fed, most were resting and watching movies, and Miss Kiki and the missis were howling together in their own little corner. We successfully made it through the flight without any physical altercations. The Lead Flight Attendant returned to the front of the cabin to resume his responsibilities for landing.

On my way to return to the back I thanked Miss Kiki's owners for joining us today and told them it was nice chatting with them. I wished them a good rest of their day and we all took our seats for landing. The plane landed and we made it to the gate. Passengers deplaned and the difficult couple blazed past the Lead Flight Attendant with rude comments under their breath about how he was the worst flight attendant they had ever experienced and how they'd be writing in their complaints. Directly following the husband and wife was the gentleman in 4D who had given up his sandwich. He passed off a note to the Lead Flight Attendant with a smile and said, "You all did a phenomenal job with some pretty challenging people. You worked well as a team and I applaud you. If you need anything, my information is on that paper."

As a crew we met to debrief the events of the flight. We talked about how the situation was handled, shared our frustrations, and discussed if there was anything that we could have done differently to avoid the conflict. We all agreed that the Lead Flight Attendant had done everything that he could and that these passengers in row 5 wouldn't have been pleased until the sandwich appeared.

I recalled all the events and some of the details and then started putting some pieces together that had snuck right past us during the flight. The wife had requested a gluten-free and dairy-free meal. Caught up in the overreaction of her husband and how quickly the whole situation escalated, none of us realized how ridiculous this request was at the time. This woman had demanded a sandwich with bread that was full of gluten and had melted cheese throughout, which was made with dairy. In fact, the cheese had melted in a way that made it inseparable from the turkey bacon and the egg. Maybe she could have taken off the bread — she didn't — but she wouldn't have been able to remove the cheese from the egg and the bacon, which also didn't seem to bother her. By that point we all just shook our heads and laughed because this woman was all shades of strange and none of us found any point in trying to make sense of her actions.

In recalling the facts of the story, the Lead Flight Attendant remembered that he had the note in his pocket from Mr. 4D. He pulled it out, opened it up as a $20 bill fell out. In addition to the money and the personal information that 4D mentioned would be inside, there was a note that read:

Lead Flight Attendant,

I just wanted to tell you that you and your crew did a great job handling this situation. I know these are the *type of people that will write bad letters to the company even though you did everything within your power to make them happy. Here's $20 to buy yourself some lunch or maybe a glass of wine after you get off work. You definitely deserve it. I know I'd need some alcohol after dealing with them. Also, all my contact information is written at the bottom in case you need a witness account of how they treated you. I'd be more than happy to explain the real story in your defense. Can you believe she took a sandwich that had a bite taken out of it already? By the way, did the wife (or Miss Kiki) mention anything to you about liking the special sauce on the sandwich? I licked the entire underside of the bread before I offered her my meal. Did you notice my seatmate laughing at me? Just a bit of karma in your honor. I hope your day gets better!*

—4D

Our eyes had bulged at the shock of finding out what 4D had done to the sandwich. We were all in complete disbelief as we nervously laughed with each other, discovering that 5C and 5D had been served a serious plate of karma. Once we arrived at the layover, we found a nearby restaurant and put the $20 to good use, each ordering a well-deserved glass of wine as our friend in 4D suggested. We gave a toast: "Here's to Miss Kiki and to Miss Karma!

Travel Tip

Always remember to take a moment to appreciate the experience of flying. You are soaring through the air in a giant metal tube with an incredible view of the billowy clouds in the sky and the beautiful landscape down below. Enjoy the ride and relax! Make new friends, be kind to each other, and keep an eye out for all the crazy, sweet, and hysterical stories that need to be told. I guarantee that you won't even have to go far to stumble upon a story that will bring humor to your day.

ACKNOWLEDGEMENTS

Thank you to my parents for their never-ending support. Specifically, I'd like to thank my mother for consistently encouraging me to write down and keep track of all the stories from my experiences. From the moment that I started my job as a teacher, she championed the idea of celebrating the humor that fell into my lap while working with children, and didn't hesitate to point out that a similar book could be written using the stories from flying. You were right, Ma. I *could* write a book someday!

Additionally, I am forever indebted to my friend Linda Weitzman, who selflessly gave of her time as my sounding board, editing angel/genius, and generally amazing friend. Your feedback, creativity, and support throughout this project inspired me. I couldn't be more grateful to have you in my life. Thank you times a million.

I'd also like to thank my family and friends for their support of my storytelling and all the wonderfully positive feedback that encouraged me to begin writing in the first place. Specifically, I'd like to thank my friend Erin Confair, for her contribution to brainstorming titles, as well as Amber Letters for believing in my work and helping to make the book a reality. I can't thank you both enough for your consistent support and cheerleading along the way.

Finally, I must thank my friend Andrea Wildason, for knowing me well enough to know that I desperately needed the encouragement to take a leap of faith into a new career. Without your guidance and love along the way, I would have never been brave enough to follow the aviation path which has been, by far, the best decision of my life. Because of you, my stories exist.